A Travelers Guide To

SOUTHWEST INDIAN ARTS AND CRAFTS

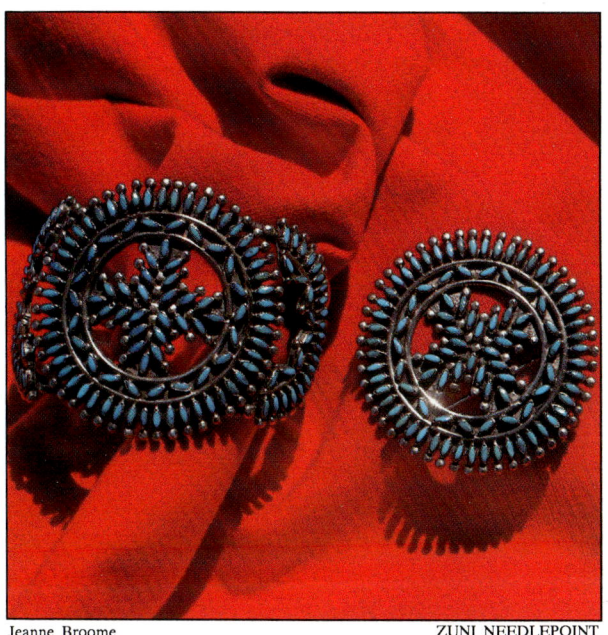

Jeanne Broome   ZUNI NEEDLEPOINT

by **CHARLOTTE SMITH NEYLAND**

A RENAISSANCE HOUSE PUBLICATION

Copyright 1992 by Charlotte Smith Neyland. Printed in the United States of America. All rights reserved. This book or any parts thereof, may not be reproduced in any manner whatsoever without written permission of the publisher:

ISBN: 1-55838-129-5

RENAISSANCE HOUSE
A Division of Jende-Hagan, Inc.
541 Oak Street ~ P.O. Box 177
Frederick, CO 80530

Cover photo of Navajo potter Faye Tso, courtesy Richard Weston Photography

10 9 8 7 6 5 4 3 2

Welcome

Southwestern native American arts and crafts date back before the time of Christ. Yet they remain a reflection of the skill, technique and artistry of their makers. The craftwork of the southwest Indians is but a small part of the vast heritage of the North American native people. Across the continent, the diverse Indian cultures have created unique artistry from textiles, clay, plants, skins, wood, stone, shells, horns, beads, metal, and feathers.

A trip to the southwestern United States offers more than a sightseeing of ancient lands and unusual geologic formations. Many regions are inhabited by natives whose ancestries date back more than 14,000 years. Like their religious ceremonies, the craftwork of these indigenous people reflects a sacred connection to the Great Spirit and the natural creation they so deeply respect. Designs, colors, styles, and materials are often traditional--handed on to new artists by grandmothers and grandfathers. Changes in art reflect these ancient traditions and embellish the pieces with a kind of permanent spirit of the past.

The best way to find that particular pot, rug, or piece of jewelry is to allow time to breathe in and digest the silent yet powerful spirit of the Indian country. Stop along the way to the next trading post and let the silence speak to you about the native people. Drink in the colors of the earth, buttes, and sky. Inhale the odors of rock and juniper. Listen to the cry of the hawk circling overhead. Touch the earth and remember the ancients who may have walked here.

Then go shopping. With the beauty of the natives' homeland in your mind, seek the piece that best captures the essence of the land, plants, animals, and sky. That piece will enlighten your life through its representation of these sacred lands of the southwest native Americans.

To learn more about southwestern arts and crafts, consult the following fine references:

Generations in Clay, A.E. Dittert, Jr. & Fred Plog
Seven Families in Pueblo Pottery, Maxwell Mus. of Anthropology
Posts and Rugs, The Story of Navajo Rugs and Their Homes, H. L. James
Indian Jewelry, Fact & Fantasy, M.M. Lund
Hopi Silver, M. Wright
Indian Silversmithing, W. Ben Hunt
Pueblo Indian Textiles, A Living Tradition, K.P. Kent
American Indian Art, magazine

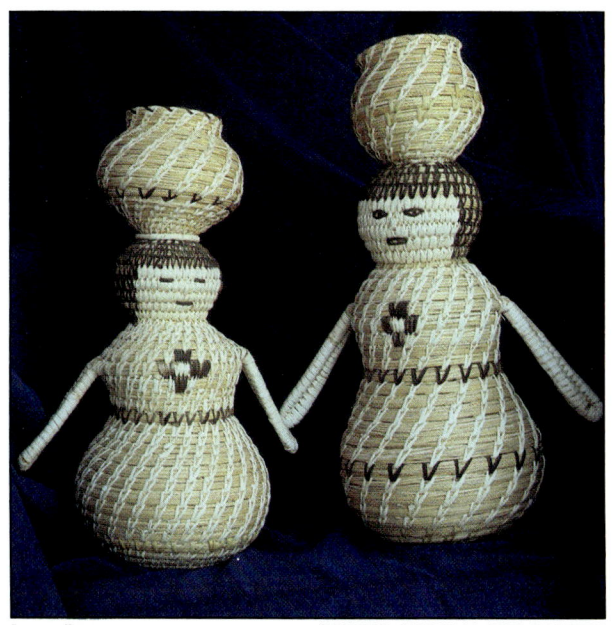

Jeanne Broome   TOHONO O'ODHAM GIRL BASKETS

CONTENTS

Welcome	2
Glossary of Craft Terms	4
Baskets	5
Rugs & Blankets	15
Map	24
How To Tell a Fake	27
Basic Tips For Buying	28
Pottery: Today & Yesterday	29
Pottery of the Southwest Pueblos	33
What Makes a Piece of Pottery Valuable?	40
Jewelry	41
Other Native Crafts	46
Indian Arts & Crafts Assn.	47
Tribal Enterprises, Co-ops, Museums	48

Our thanks to Mr. Barton Wright, Ethnologist, for his careful reading of the text and preview of the photos prior to publication.

GLOSSARY OF CRAFT TERMS

Pottery Terms

MATTE BLACK-ON-BLACK: A design painted on a slip, then smothered with manure in a fire to carbonize the clay black.

BLACK-ON-WHITE: Black, painted on a white slip.

COILING: A method of forming pottery by making rope-like coils stacked to build up the walls of a piece.

POLISHING: Rubbing of the slip with a worn stone until the finish is smooth and lustrously shiny.

POLYCHROME: Use of three or more colors on a pot.

REDWARE: Pottery made of yellow clay which fires in an oxidizing atmosphere.

SCRAPING AND SANDING: Scraping is done with a tool made from a gourd to smooth the coils and even out the walls of a pot. Sanding with a fine grade paper, is done when the pot is dry to prepare the surface for slip and polishing.

SGRAFFITO: Scratching through the slip to expose the color of the clay underneath. Some contemporary potters achieve this effect after the firing.

SHERDS: *(Shards)* Broken pieces of pottery.

SLIP: A finer grade of clay with the consistency of cream which is used to color the surface of a pot or change the surface texture.

TEMPER: Any coarse material added to clay to even the drying and workability. Temper lessens the temperature shock in firing. Sand, ground sherds, and ground rock are commonly used.

Jewelry Terms

APPLIQUE: Silverworking technique using solder to fasten one layer of metal to another.

BEZEL: A thin band of silver which surrounds and holds a stone in place.

CABOCHON: A stone which has not been cut in facets but is rounded on the top.

CAST: Melting and pouring silver or gold into a mold or form. Four common methods of casting include:
  Cement - pressing a piece of jewelry into wet cement mixed with motor oil to form the impression into which silver is poured. **Centrifugal** - spinning a hollow mold by high speed machine, and forcing silver into the cavity. **Sand Cast** - a mold carved from sandstone into which silver is poured. **Tufa Cast** - same as sand-casting, except that the mold is carved from tufastone, a porous, pumice-like rock.

CONCHA: *(Concho)* Meaning "shell", a round, oval, square, or rectangular piece of silver, threaded in multiples on a leather strap and worn as a belt.

FACETS: One side of a many sided cut stone.

NAJA: *(Najabe)* A crescent pendant at the bottom of Squash Blossom necklaces.

PAWN: The name given to the economic system begun in the 1870s by which Indians could use jewelry as collateral for money or supplies given them by the traders. The term is also applied to jewelry acquired by the traders when the Indian owner failed to redeem it.

SQUASH BLOSSOM: A Navajo or Zuni style necklace incorporating flower-like beads with flanges of plain silver or set with stones.

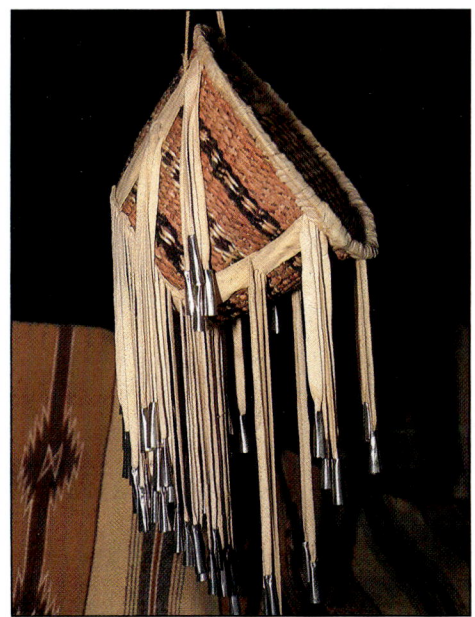

Jeanne Broome   SAN CARLOS APACHE BURDEN BASKET

BASKETS

"One day Coyote climbed a hill and sat down to watch the world go by. Suddenly a lovely girl came walking by and he knew this was the girl he wanted to marry. Strangely, the girl wasn't carrying her burden basket on her back, it was walking along by itself after her. Yet a basket never walks around on its own. It seems that this girl's father was a powerful medicine man and had made this basket especially for his daughter."

"The lovely girl was gathering firewood, which she loaded into the basket. She gathered a great deal of wood, and when she was finished she turned to go home, and the basket followed her."

"Coyote was thinking of getting that basket and showing people how smart he was so he said, 'Hahaha. So the burden basket walks around.' The basket just stopped where it was and became a mountain which the people now call Quijo Toa (Burden Basket) Mountain.*"

Southwest Indian baskets date back several thousand years and were created for carrying, storing, cooking and processing food. Depending on size and shape, they functioned as household or as ceremonial vessels. Baskets used for storing grain, for example, had wide

---

*From **Legends and Lore of the Papago and Pima Indians,** by Dean & Lucille Saxton

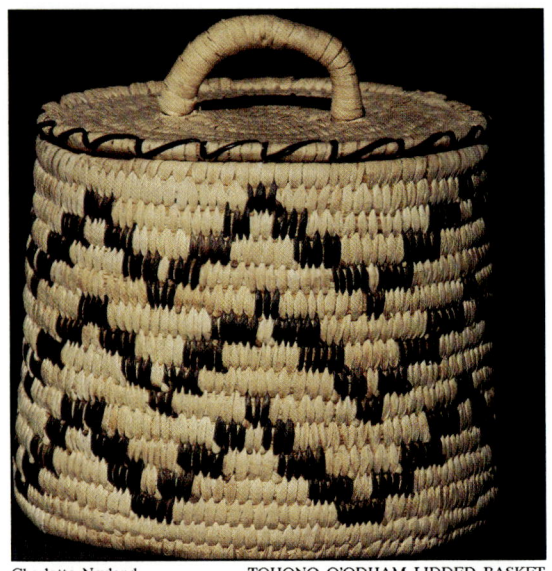

Charlotte Neyland   TOHONO O'ODHAM LIDDED BASKET

mouths while those for water had narrow mouths. Water jars were lined with pitch or fruit pulp to prevent leakage.

Because it was transported on the carrier's back, the burden basket was woven into a bucket or conical shape. Other early styles resembled trays or wastebaskets. These, along with the later lidded forms and other variations are still made by today's native Americans.

Three basic techniques are applied in weaving baskets--coiling, plaiting, and twining. The style and design created by the different techniques is a good way to identify a particular tribe's baskets. Before starting, a weaver decides which portion of the basket will be decorated and how the pattern will be arranged. The design is organized in the weaver's mind. Ornamental beads, tin tinklers, buckskin, and feathers are sometimes part of the organization of the basket. The style of the basket that makes it uniquely Apache, Hopi, Navajo, or Pima, evolves as the weaver works. Designs may include dots, lines, squares, rectangles, circles, triangles, diamonds, steps, frets, and meanders.

Plants used by the southern tribes may be left in their natural colors or dyed with commercial or homemade dyes. Black is extracted from devil's claw (martynia); red from yucca, mountain mahogany, or sumac; and yellow from rabbitbrush, cedar ashes, and yucca.

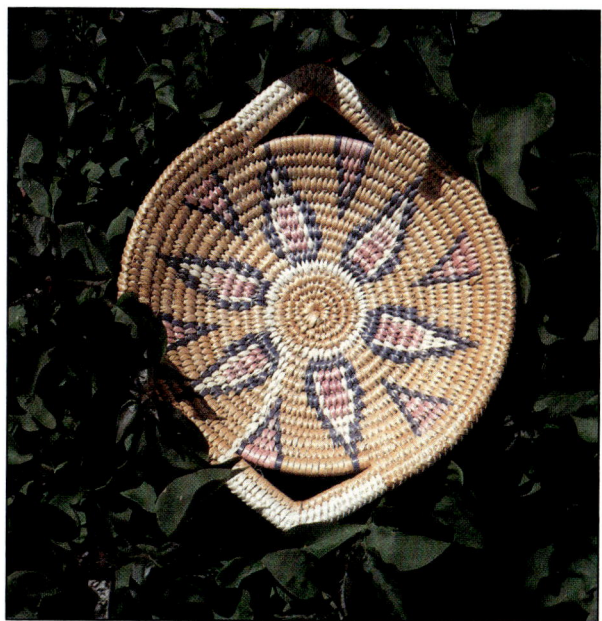

Jeanne Broome JICARILLA APACHE BASKET

Apache & Yavapai
(Ah-PATCH-ee and YAV-ah-pie)

Now located many miles apart, these tribes once occupied lands adjacent to each other in Arizona. The Apache live near the easterly White Mountains while the Yavapai now live near Prescott, Arizona.

Apache and Yavapai baskets are so similar that distinguishing the two is difficult. Size, stitching and coil counts are generally comparable. Designers from both tribes use circles, diamonds, crosses, triangles, zigzags, stars, flowers, coyote tracks, and swastikas. Some of these basketmakers also weave in life forms of men and women, dogs, horses, deer, birds, gila monsters, and saguaro cacti. Using various wood--shoots of willow, cottonwood, rabbit brush and devil's claw, the Apache and Yavapai weavers usually weave the basket in a circle moving from right to left. Other tribes may weave from left to right.

The distinguishing characteristics of these baskets lie in the design and weaving. The Apache put more designs on one basket, sometimes giving a cluttered appearance. Yavapai weave with more space between designs, creating a simpler effect.

Havasupai (Have-ah-SUE-pie)

Located in the Cataract Canyon of the Colorado River, 2,400 feet below the plateau, the Havasupai

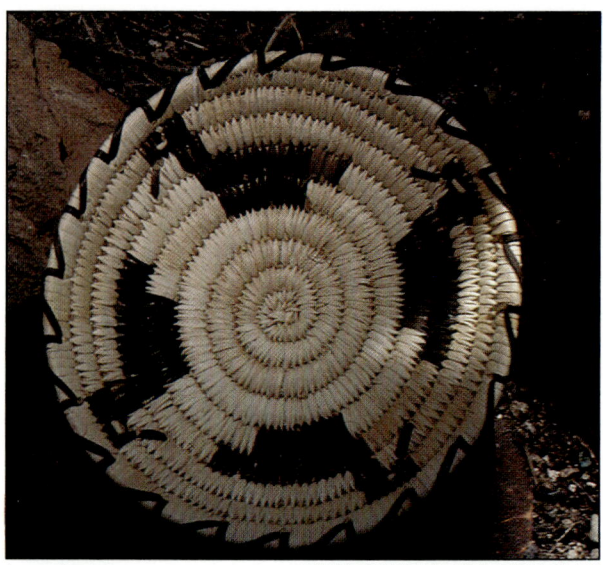

Jeanne Broome   DUCK DESIGN FROM DEVIL'S CLAW

people dwell along the fertile, Eden-like Havasu Creek. Here the weavers gather cat's-claw, cottonwood, and willow used for twining, and squawberry and Apache plume for twining and coiling. Leaving the seclusion of their canyon floor homes, they may ride horseback up to the rim and gather cat's-claw.

Trays and bowls are twined and coiled. Burden baskets are formed from conical twining. Jars, which are not common today, were biconically formed and pitched. These looked like a woven, round pyramid, carried with the point downward.

Crafters usually cover the base of a carrying basket with rawhide and weave the handles of horsehair. The latter is also used for handles on water bottles. Cooked peach or apricot and pinon pitch provide waterproofing.

Natural dyes are extracted from berry and holly grape root to create walnut brown and gold colors. Red-brown comes from the Spanish bayonet root, and black from devil's claw. Indigo plant is the source for yellow, orange, pink, and green. Havasupai baskets may be mistaken for ones created by the Yavapai who use a similar coiling technique and design.

Some say that modern baskets do not compare with the older ones produced in the 1920s and 30s. These high quality creations were complex in design and tightly coiled, some with 6 to 7 coils and 15 to 19 stitches per inch. But as more buyers demand better quality, it is hoped the Supai weavers will return to their former tradition of refinement and sophistication.

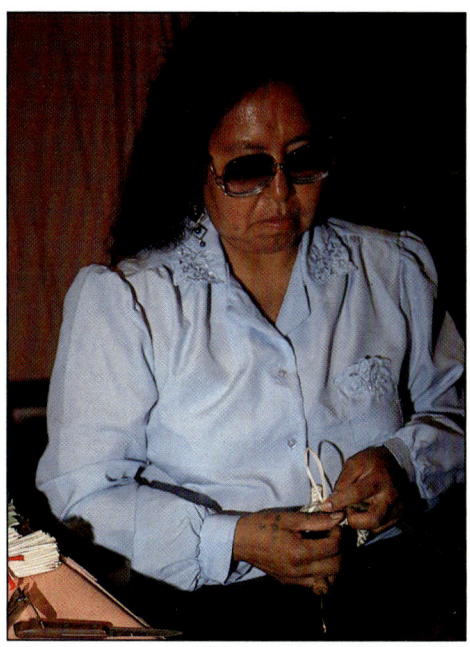
Jeanne Broome   TOHONO O'ODHAM BASKETMAKER

Hualapai (Walapai) (WALL-ah-pie)

Closely related to the Havasupai are the Hualapai, who were originally one tribe with them. Today the two intermarry, sharing different aspects of their cultures. The main differences between the two groups stems from the resources found in the areas where they live.

Unlike the Havasupai--agricultural people who live in a fertile valley--the Hualapai dwell in a desert grassland west of their Supai neighbors. They make their living in cattle raising, forestry, and light industry. Sumac and willow provide the materials for their baskets. Among the early Hualapai baskets were seedbeaters which were used to knock ripe seeds from standing grass stems. The Hualapai also made cradleboards, carriers which strapped to the back for holding an infant.

Burden baskets are made from cottonwood, willow, sumac, and mulberry, but most weavers' preferences are cat's-claw (acacia) and strawberry sumac. Craftsmen use a twill or diagonal twining technique which involves a textile-like process of interweaving materials and incorporates plain bands for decoration. At the bottom are rawhide patches to protect the baskets. They are pitched with hard, dried coatings of yucca fibers, mescal pulp, and stewed peaches.

Water bottles are twined, coarsely woven, coated

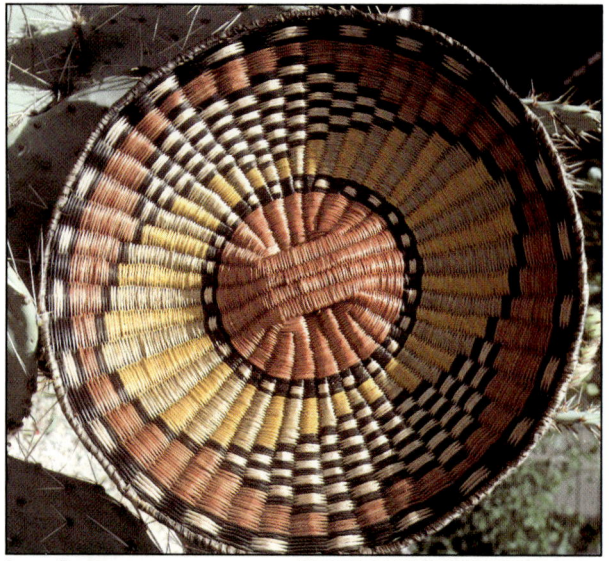
Jeanne Broome   WICKER BASKET FROM THIRD MESA

with pine pitch and yucca fibers. The bottles have flat bottoms and are globular or pear-shaped, 8 to 9 inches high. Biconical bottles average 15 inches high and 10 to 12 inches in diameter. Carrying loops are of horsehair or yucca.

Seed beaters usually are plain and made of sumac rods. These rods are woven into narrow, elongated spoon shapes, bent into tight arcs and brought back to form rough, bound handles. They look somewhat like a woven, oblong tennis racket with a short handle. A typical Hualapai basket is a twined, deep bowl with slightly rounded sides, a flat bottom, and thick flat rims. Colors are black, russet, green, brown and red.

Hopi (HO-pee)

Among the Pueblo tribes, the Hopi are the most productive basketmakers. Their reservation is surrounded by the vast Navajoland of northeastern Arizona. Three mesas--First, Second and Third--make up the Hopi homeland. Baskets made on Second and Third Mesas differ according to the weaver's mesa home. Common designs are kachinas (a figure representing an ancestral spirit), deer, lightning, eagles, cloud and other significant Hopi figures.

Second Mesa baskets are traditionally coiled of galleta grass (a desert and dry plains species), and yucca, using vegetal dyes. The material is woven into a swirl or spiral formation moving from right to left. Prehistoric basketmakers wove the natural gray and white into plaques and deep baskets. Yellow was

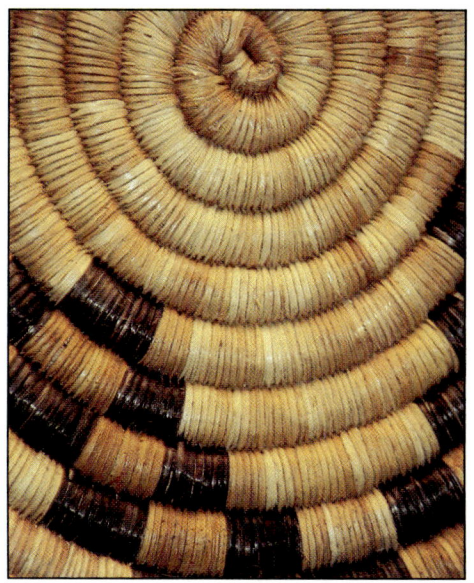

Charlotte Neyland   HOPI PLAQUE, SECOND MESA

achieved by freezing plant strips in snow and drying them in the sun.

The people of Third Mesa create plaited wicker baskets in bright colors, very popular with travelers and natives alike. Sumac and rabbitbrush are colored with vegetal and aniline dyes. Plaited yucca sifters (for straining out heated sand used to parch corn) and rectangular trays are also part of Third Mesa art.

Because they are given as gifts, Second Mesa baskets are sometimes found on Third Mesa and vice versa. An important social currency, plaques are often given as paybacks or gifts. In a Hopi marriage, for example, blue corn piki bread is piled high on a plaque and taken by the prospective bride and her mother to the groom's mother when marriage negotiations begin.

A groom's plaque is designed of yucca in colors of natural, sun bleached white, green, and black. This plaque must never be sold, for upon the groom's death, his spirit needs the plaque to go safely to the Underworld, the place where life is believed to continue after death.

While many baskets are made expressly for sale, others have been used in ritual or social ways that reinforce relationships in the Hopi world. A plaque or basket may be used in ceremony or as a payback like currency and later sold to a tourist.

Navajo (NAV-ah-ho)

Before 1900, Navajo women made three types of

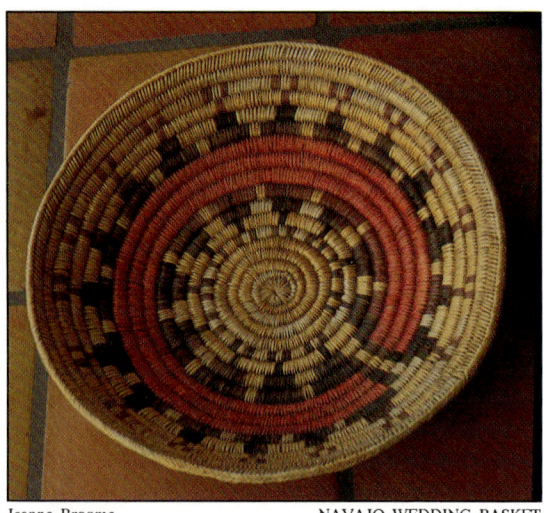

Jeanne Broome NAVAJO WEDDING BASKET

baskets. *Tsii'zis* were twined or coiled burden baskets used for collecting food. *Toshjeeh* were coiled jars, coated inside and out with pinon pitch and used for carrying water. *Ts'aa'* were coiled trays. But by the turn of the century, basket making was almost unknown. In the 1960s the craft began a revival and today many kinds of baskets are produced.

The coiled tray is still used in rituals, for food processing, holding, and storage. The most familiar of these is the wedding basket design used in wedding ceremonies and to hold religious paraphernalia of sacred corn meal, herbs, and yucca seeds.

The white center of the wedding basket represents Earth Mother or the beginning of life. Stepped terrace figures are symbols of clouds or mountains, and the red circular band represents sunrays or the rainbow. A distinctive break in the pattern is called the *'atlin* (road or pathway) and is required for ceremonial use. It symbolizes the emergence myth, the creation story of the Navajo people, and acts as an entrance or exit for supernatural powers. It also orients the basket in the ritual easterly direction from which the power of the creator or god is believed to originate.

The pitch-jar is another popular item. Shaped like a jar with a large base, these baskets are sealed with pinon or pine pitch to prevent leakage. Burden baskets, once used by every household, are now rare, having been replaced by metal and plastic.

Navajo basketmakers study other weavers' work, consult publications on basketry, and observe nature when creating new designs. To keep the art alive, collectors are urged to appreciate the new and distinctive designs of non-traditional forms and

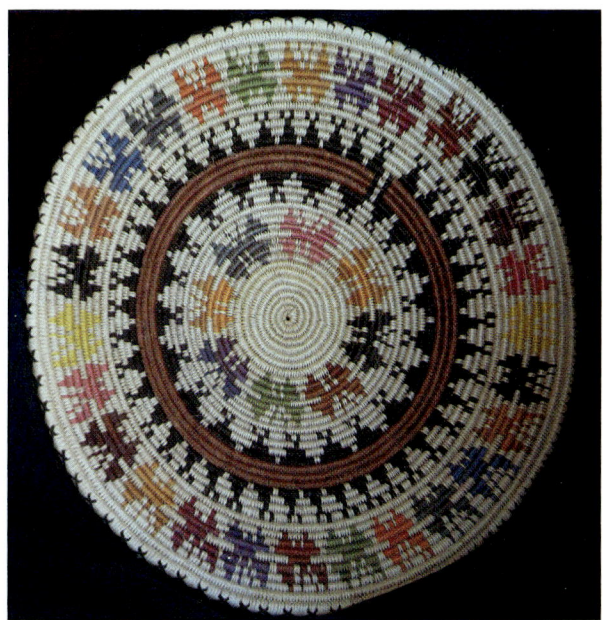

Jeanne Broome — PAIUTE MULTI-COLORED BUTTERFLIES

encourage weavers to create them.

San Juan Paiute (San Wan PIE-ute)

In their homeland in southern Utah and northern Arizona, the San Juan Paiutes gather yucca, sumac, and willow to create the baskets they sell to Navajos, traders, and craft dealers. Baskets are a steady source of income for these weavers. Old style baskets are made with the same skill and beauty as were those of the mothers and grandmothers. Filling the trading post shelves are modern wedding basket designs, original Paiute patterns, and interpretations from other tribes. Baskets are colored with vegetal and commercial dyes.

Seed beaters, coiled parching trays (used to sift hot sand for parched corn), coiled bowls, cradles, and burden baskets are still made today. Wedding basket designs may relate to nature or pictorial traditions of the various tribes. Sizes range from three inches or less to jumbo baskets measuring 56 inches.

Gathered when the plants are dormant and fibers are stronger, in spring or late fall, the materials are stored and later soaked to restore pliability to the fibers. Similarities to Pai (Yavapai, Hualapai, and Havasupai) crafts are found in the conical burden baskets and utilitarian trays. The Paiute pitched water bottles also resemble those made by the Navajo and Apache tribes.

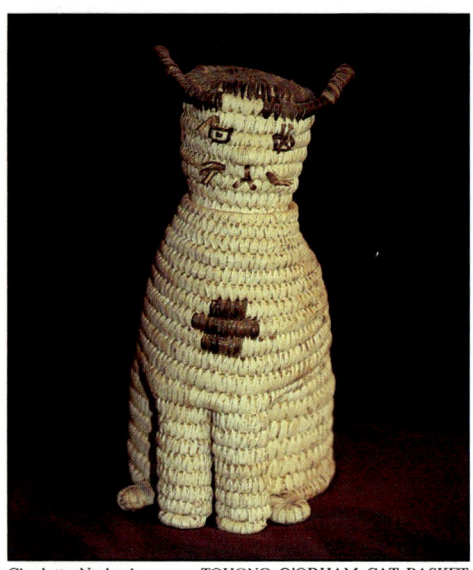
Charlotte Neyland — TOHONO O'ODHAM CAT BASKET

Tohono O'Odham & Pima
(TO-na O TA-hm and PEE-ma)

From their reservation home west of Tucson, the Tohono O'odham (Papago) produce a greater variety of baskets than any other southwest tribe. Forms include trays, bowls, animals, birds, humans, jars, wastebaskets, plaques, coasters, and miniatures.

While most of the work is done by women, baskets created from metal are made primarily by men using recycled hay baling wire. An average basket contains about 100 feet of wire. Shapes of the metal creations are similar to those of other baskets but also include plants, flowers, reptiles and insects.

Repetition in the design of natural fiber baskets is characteristic of Tohono O'odham work. Among the popular materials are agave fibers, ocotillo, mesquite bark, arrow bush for crude bird's nest baskets, and wheat straw on occasion. Traditional willow and devil's claw coiled baskets so closely resemble traditional Pima baskets they are difficult to tell apart.

Pima baskets, once made with fine stitching and complex decorative patterns are a rare find today. Pima weavers used willow and cattails to create a coiled basket that is now, unfortunately, a thing of the past. Wheat-straw baskets, some large enough to sit in, are also a lost art. Coiled and miniature baskets are still made by a few women and some weave horsehair. Because fewer Pima women are weaving, their artistry may soon be lost.

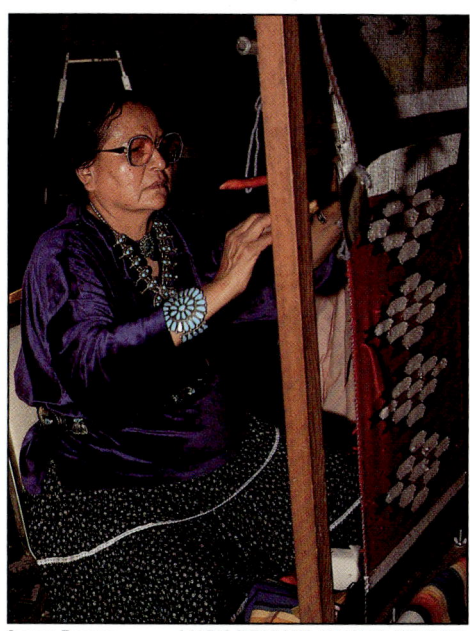

Jeanne Broome MARY DERRICK, NAVAJO WEAVER

Rugs and Blankets

SONG OF THE SKY LOOM

O our Mother the Earth, O our Father the Sky,
Your children are we, and with tired backs
We bring you the gifts that you love.
Then weave for us a garment of brightness;
May the warp be the white light of morning,
May the weft be the red light of evening,
May the fringes be the falling rain,
May the border be the standing rainbow.
Thus weave for us a garment of brightness
That we may walk fittingly where birds sing,
That we may walk fittingly where grass is green,
O our Mother the Earth, O our Father the Sky!*

One feels a certain ambience upon entering a room arrayed in Navajo rugs. Maybe it's the spirit of the weaver or the materials. Perhaps the vibrant colors and patterns fill a latent need for warmth within us. Whatever the cause, a bond is built between the viewer and the woven art.

Weavings are not only *objets d'art*, they represent a culture. Over the years, Navajo weavings have changed in design, materials, and usage. But they remain, as in old times, expressions of the individuals and the communities in which they are woven.

---

*Invocation from the Tewa Pueblos

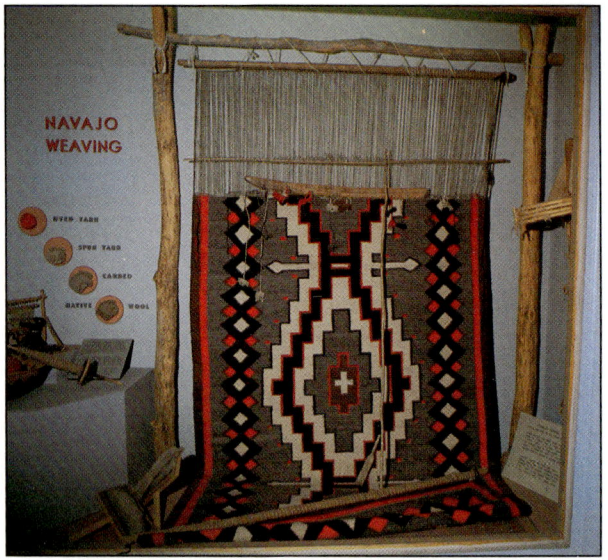

Jeanne Broome   NAVAJO WEAVERS' TOOLS

The earliest looms probably consisted of a supporting stick or stake to which fibrous twine was tied. The warp was suspended from a central point and a small stick used to tighten the fibers. Materials were probably horsehair, buffalo hair, or strings of plant fiber.

Since the stake offered only one point of support, a mat could not be woven upon it. The supporting frame evolved of necessity. By placing two stakes near each other and suspending a third one across them, a mat could be woven. This single device created the warp rack upon which plaiting, twining, twilling, and their variations could be practiced.

This weaving frame had its limitations. Warp strings dangled and tangled easily. To solve this problem some weavers balled the fiber into membrane bags to prevent tangling. By bagging the loose ends, they produced a weighted warp while keeping the materials clean. Looms with rigid warps are thought to have begun with the northwest coast Salishan people who used all-wool material.

Another loom, called the belt or waist type, was suspended from a branch or pole so the weaver could work at an angle convenient to the hands while weaving diagonally. The free end was tied around the crafter's waist and drawn taut while working. Usually the weaver was seated on the ground. Cotton was generally the fiber of choice.

The Navajo loom of today is as aboriginal as it was in the early days. Its counterpart would be the prehistoric Pueblo loom dating to the 10th century. Called the vertical loom, it consists of a supporting

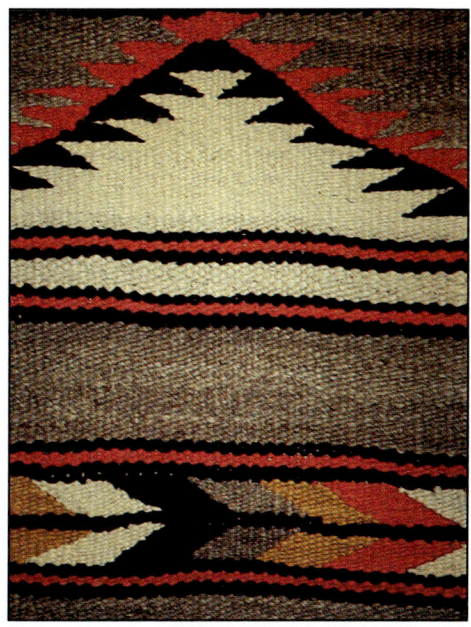

Charlotte Neyland   TYPICAL REASONABLY PRICED RUG

frame and numerous poles, often hung with ropes, to permit mobility in weaving.

Early weaving materials included yucca, native hemp, milkweed, bark fibers, animal hair and fur, human hair, and feathers. Dyes and colors of the earlier weavings were natural white, brown, gray, tan, and black. Vegetal dyes produced colors of rust, yellow, and green. Indigo blue was introduced by the Spanish explorers to the Southwest. Red was acquired in later years when the Navajo traded with the Spanish for bolts of wool cloth called *baize*. The Indians unraveled this felt-like material and respun it, then wove it into combinations with the sheep's wool.

Navajo weaving is divided into six periods. The Early Classic (1700-1850), marks the time of advancement of the Spanish into Indian lands. The Navajo are said to have learned the art of weaving from the Pueblo who lived in their territory after fleeing from the invading Spanish in the late 1600s. Simple weaving produced shirts, dresses, shoulder blankets, ponchos, and leggings. Wool was acquired from sheep introduced by the Spanish explorers.

The Classic Period (1850-1863) brought the Navajo economic success with their trade of men's shoulder blankets to military leaders, Ute, and other Indian tribes. Called Chief Blankets, these weavings were patterned in black, brown, or blue and white horizontal bands. Later designs in this period included diamonds and checks in red, yellow and green. Even during their

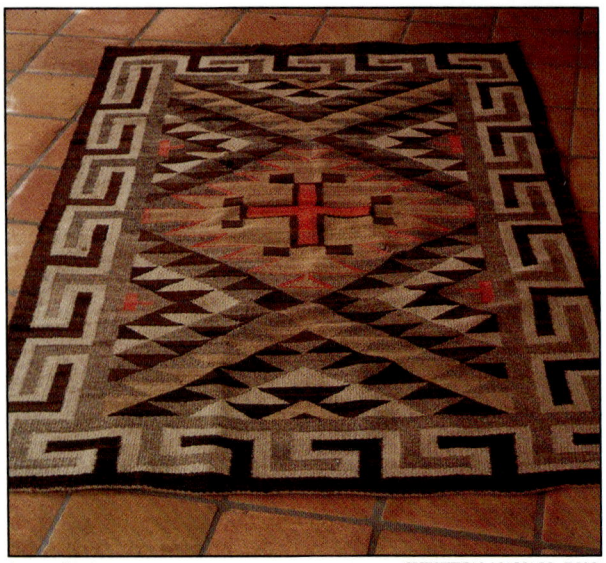

Jeanne Broome   WESTERN NAVAJO RUG

1863 imprisonment by the government at Bosque Redondo in east-central New Mexico, weavers continued to produce blankets of roving, a twisted roll of fiber, having been deprived of their native wool resources.

The release of the Navajo people in 1868 began the Transition Period (1868-1890). They continued to weave with commercial yarn, producing blankets of bright and varied colors. Hence the craft went into another period of change.

The late 1800s brought the beginning of the Rug Period (1890-1920). When traders introduced machine-made Pendletons onto the reservation, the Navajo stopped making blankets and began weaving heavier, larger pieces which the white man bought for floor coverings. Juan Lorenzo Hubbell of Ganado, Arizona, and John B. Moore of Crystal, New Mexico, were great influences on the growth of the Navajo rug as art. Hubbell discouraged the use of inferior dyes and loose weaving, persuading craftsmen to create the old designs-- bold crosses, stripes, and diamonds in deep red aniline backgrounds bordered in black. Thus the Ganado style of weaving began.

Moore had weavers bring in raw wool which he sent to eastern mills for cleaning and dyeing. His design ideas combined traditional Navajo and geometric figures. He published a small catalog describing the weavings and began a successful mail order business. It was Moore's patterns that later gave rise to the regional style rug called the Two Gray Hills (p.23). Crystal regional rugs (p.22) also evolved at this time.

Despite these developments, another decline

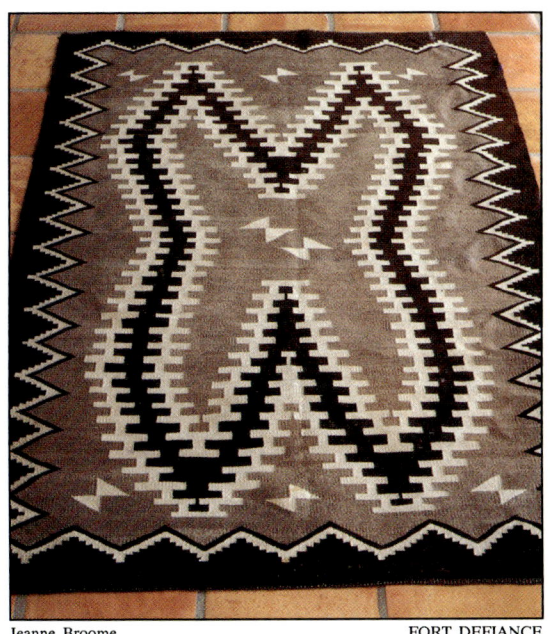

Jeanne Broome　　　　　　　　　　FORT DEFIANCE

occurred in the early 1900s when the government introduced flocks of French Rambouillet sheep to the Navajo reservation. While the animals produced large quantities of wool and mutton, the weaving material was inferior. Wool was short and oily so rugs became heavy and coarse. The colors were inconsistent due to the women's inability to remove the grease from the wool. Since traders bought rugs by the pound, Navajo women left dirt in the wool to increase the weight. And so weaving took a downturn.

The Revival Period (1920-1940) ushered in a rejuvenation of the craft. Leon H. McSparron, of Chinle Trading Post, and Mary C. Wheelwright, a Navajo benefactress, encouraged Navajo weavers to use the old vegetal dye methods. Chinle weavers developed their regional style of pastel browns, golds, and greens. Patterns were simple stripes and bands on borderless rugs. Highly concentrated commercial dyes were created by Lucy C. Cabot, a dye expert from Boston who worked with DuPont Chemical to manufacture a special weaving dye. Weavers liked the beautiful yarns that allowed flexibility in tones. Demand led to the Diamond Dye Company's "Old Navajo" series, a packaged product that eliminated the need for weavers having to mix dangerous chemicals.

At Wide Ruin Trading Post, the William Lippincotts assisted weavers with color selection which resulted in the style that carries the post's name. This advance, along with two other important programs, created a

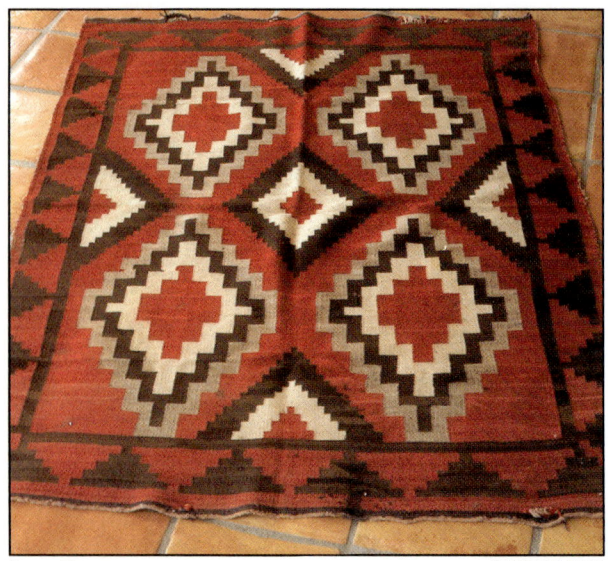

Jeanne Broome   GANADO RED

great demand for Navajo rugs. In 1934 the Navajo Sheep Breeding Laboratory was established at Fort Wingate, New Mexico. Programs were designed to cross breed New Zealand Corriedale and Merino to produce the best wool. The new breed produced a finer fleece. In 1941 the Navajo Arts and Crafts Guild was formed at Window Rock, Arizona. This group provided quality control and protection for the Indian weavers as well as assistance in acquiring good materials and fair markets.

The present era--called the Regional Style Period-- began about 1940. Building on the already existing regions at Ganado, Crystal, Chinle, and Wide Ruin new rugs became associated with specific locations on the Reservation. Today these are Shiprock, Teec Nos Pos, Lukachukai, Two Gray Hills, and Western Reservation. The best way to discover modern Navajo rugs is to visit these areas. While much of the Navajo Reservation is located in northeastern Arizona, it does extend into Utah and New Mexico as well.

Ganado (Gaa-NOD-oh) *"Herd of cattle"*

The Navajo rugs best known to non-Indians can be found east of the Hopi mesas and the Betu-Defiance Plateau in the regions near Fort Defiance, Arizona. Many collectors say the Ganado rug is what a Navajo rug should look like. Geometric crosses, diamonds and stripes in white, gray, black, and red are the hallmarks of Ganado. Rugs will vary within the region, from more complicated design and patterns to those that are less

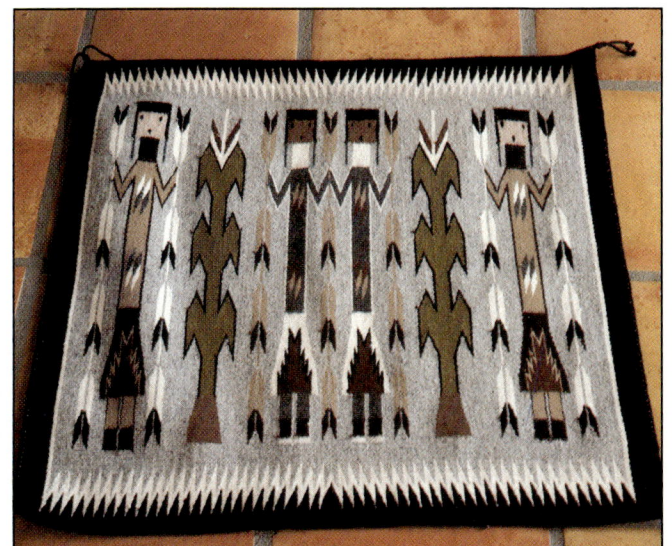

Jeanne Broome   MODERN YEI RUG

red and more black, or have serrated diamonds.

Many trading posts dot this region. Hubbell, Keams Canyon, Lower Greasewood, Pinon, Steamboat Rock, and Wood Springs carry the well-known Ganado weavings.

<u>Shiprock</u> Yei (Yea) - *Named for the nearby natural rock formation*

Shiprock is located near the San Juan River in extreme northwestern New Mexico. Yei or Yeibichai (YEA-ba-shay) rugs are small to moderate in size and bordered. Yeibechai is the name given to one or more of the Navajo divinities. Trading posts in this area are the Shiprock Trading Company, Bernard, Cove, Russell Foutz Indian Room at Farmington, Hogback, and Red Rock Trading Post.

<u>Lukachukai</u> (LOOK-a-choo-ki) *"White patch of reeds extends out"*

The Yei figures in the Lukachukai rugs might be thought of as gods dancing in the mountains. This area is near the eastern Arizona border southeast of Round Rock, near the Navajo community of Tsaile. The figures are more human in form than the Yeibechai. These larger rugs are usually woven with a background of red, gray, black or brown. You'll find them at the Lukachukai, Round Rock, Totso, and Upper Greasewood Trading Posts.

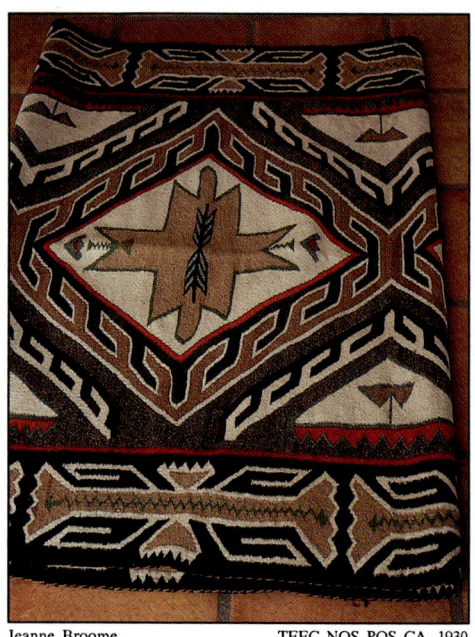

Jeanne Broome   TEEC NOS POS CA. 1930

<u>Teec Nos Pos</u> (Tea-NOSS-Poss) *"Circle of Cottonwoods"*

    The gateway to the Four Corners Monument in northeastern Arizona is home to the Teec Nos Pos weavers. Some consider their rugs to be the "least Navajo" of all regional styles. They are tightly woven and quite busy in their design. Displaying more of a Persian style, the bright colors are used in small amounts with contrasting color outlining the main pattern of serrated diamonds, zigzags, triangles and boxes. Teec Nos Pos rugs are popular among collectors because of the bright and intricate designs. Trading Posts in this area are the Beclabito, Mexican Water, Red Mesa, Sweetwater and Teec Nos Pos.

Crystal

    Crystal style rugs are woven in an area located on the west side of the Chuska Mountains in New Mexico. These beautiful and distinctive rugs are borderless, done in rich earth tones of gold, orange, brown and soft gray, green and maroon. Designs are created with wavy lines by alternating two or three wefts (horizontal or crosswise elements) of different colors. Although the Crystal Trading Post no longer exists, these rugs can be found at Hubbell Trading Post and other area locations.

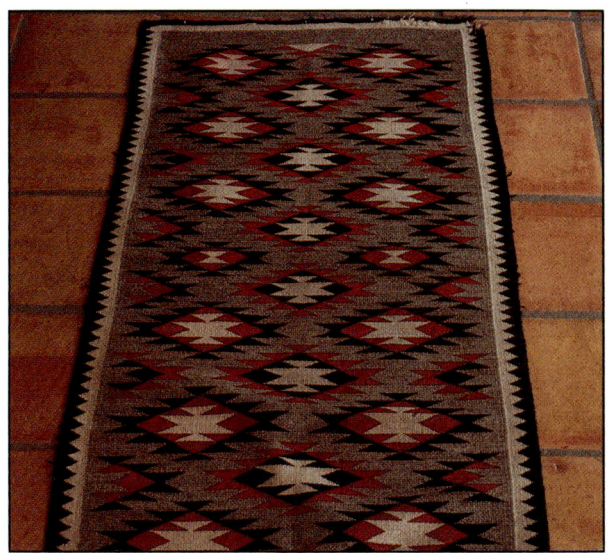

Jeanne Broome   WIDE RUIN, CA. 1930

Two Gray Hills

Located south and west of Newcomb, New Mexico, this region is home of the highly coveted Two Gray Hills rugs which sell for high prices. A small one brings at least $7,000. Woven of finely spun yarns, these rugs show a narrow line break in the border known as the spirit trail. The intent of this line is to ensure that the weaver's energy will not be trapped within the border but will follow the line out.

Usually bordered in black, these finest of all the Navajo textile weavings are designed with natural tones of blended white, black and brown. Complex multiple geometric designs add to their distinctive and delicate appearance. Two Gray Hills weavers occasionally use colors of pale yellow, red and brown, made from aniline dyes. Travelers can find these rugs in many places. Little Water, Newcomb, Sanostee, Toadlena and Two Gray Hills Trading Posts are a few locations.

Chinle (Chin-LEE) *"It Flows from the Canyon"*

Designed with squash blossoms and terraces, the Chinle borderless rugs are woven in a natural white wool background with rose, yellow, and sometimes green, brown, and gray. Perhaps these lovely creations are inspired by the beautiful Canyon de Chelly area in which they are woven. In some ways they are similar to those created at Crystal and Wide Ruin (p.22, 26) regions. Canyon de Chelly--meaning "rock canyon"--is home to Cottonwood, Garcia, Many Farms, Nazlini,

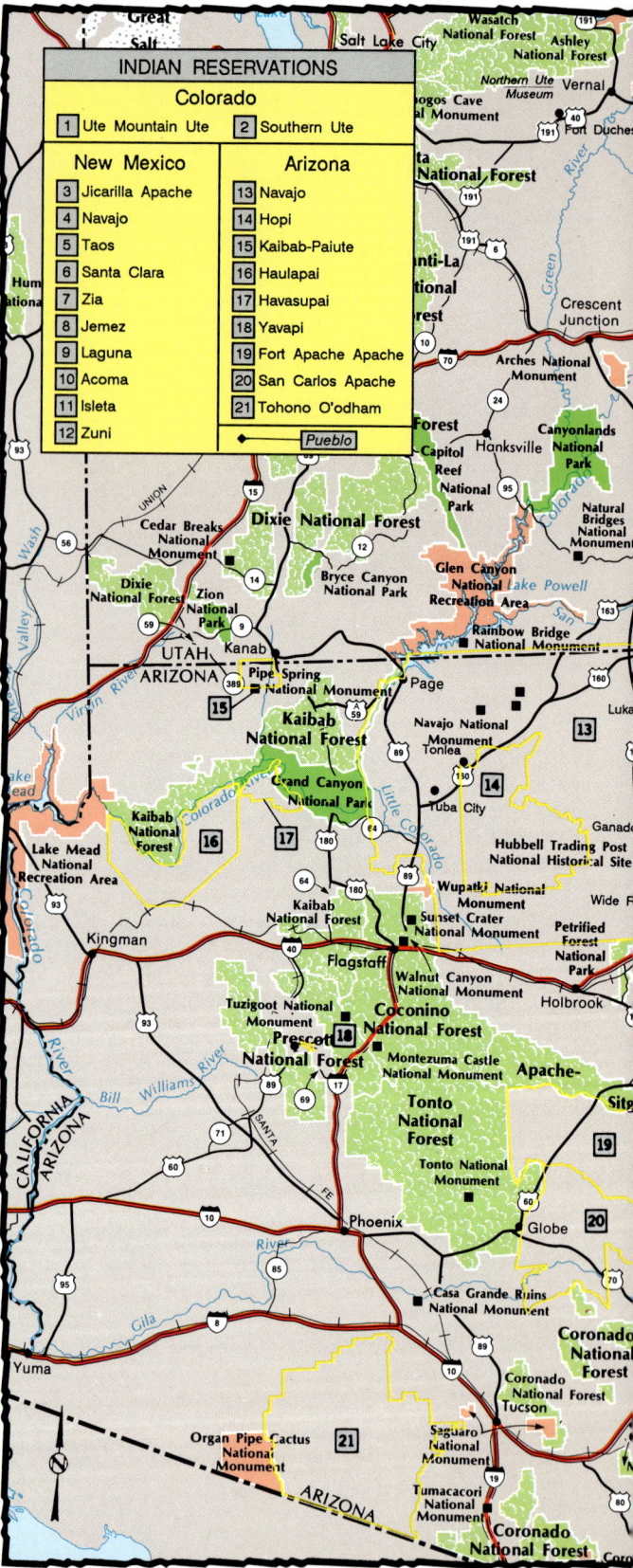

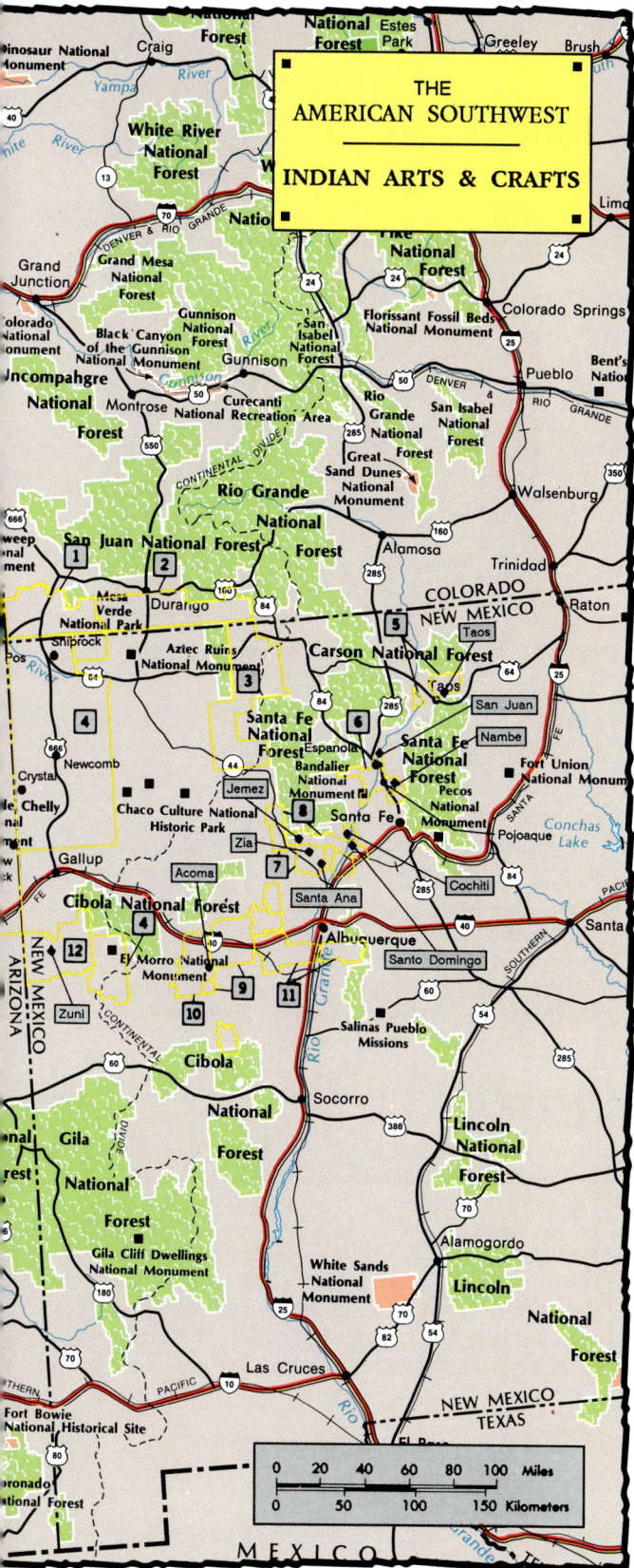

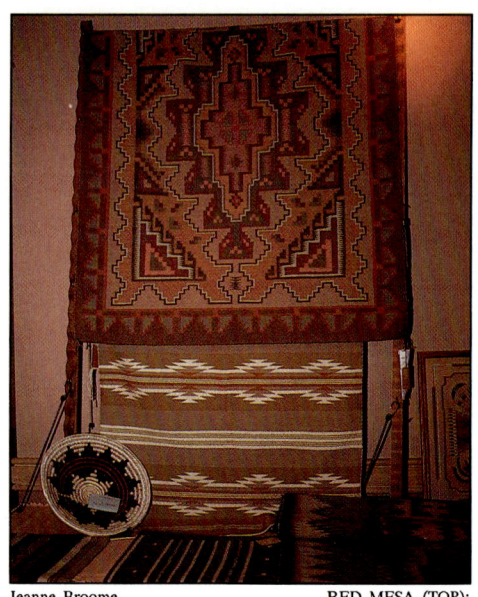

Jeanne Broome

RED MESA (TOP);
PINE SPRINGS BENEATH IT
WITH NAVAJO WEDDING BASKET TO LEFT

Salina and Thunderbird Lodge trading posts and DeChelly Galleries, Inc.

Wide Ruin

Nestled in the juniper-forested hill country between Chinle Valley and the Rio Puerco in Arizona, are the Wide Ruin weavers. These crafters work with pastels of pink, yellow, deep coral, beige, lilac, gray, brown, olive green, and tan. Stripes and bands across a borderless rug set off the panel of designs such as arrows, chevrons, and squash blossoms. Burnt Water trading post carries many local weavers' creations.

Tonalea (TAHN-lee-ah) *"Where water comes from"*

Here at the Red Lake Trading Post in the western Navajo reservation, the famous Storm Pattern rugs can be found. Their symmetrical designs are bordered and have square or rectangular centers with zigzag lines radiating to the four corners. At the corners, more squares are set. Zigzags, diamonds, arrows, and other designs are often included in the weaving. Among the area trading posts that carry Storm Pattern rugs are Cameron, Cedar Ridge, Cow Springs, Inscription House, Shonto, The Gap, Red Lake and Tuba City.

How To Tell A Fake

Replicas of Navajo rugs woven in Mexico may be nice to look at and useful as area rugs. But the serious buyer must differentiate between the authentic and the imitation. Labels are not reliable indicators of fake rugs. They may read "Genuine Navajo Made," "Genuine Indian Made," and "Genuine Indian Maid." Even some traders cannot tell the difference.

The basic differences between Navajo and Mexican rugs originate with the stringing of the looms. Mexican looms are strung horizontally. The warp yarn is cut at both ends of the rug with the ends worked back into the weaving sometimes as much as four inches. The shuttle is thrown and shed rods are operated by foot petals.

Navajos weave on a vertical loom. The warp is never cut. The rug is woven to the end and the ends are finished with a needle. The entire rug is hand woven on a hand operated loom and then hand beaten. "Lazy lines" or occasional weaving is also indicative of the true Navajo rug.

To determine whether a rug is genuine, smell it. Fibers in natural rugs have an odor because of the lanolin in sheep's wool. A wool rug will smell like a sheep. Mexican weavings--which lack the odor--are chemically treated and lighter weight than true Navajo rugs of the same size. But there's an exception. Some Navajo weavings are made of commercial yarn or are chemically cleaned. These processes produce rugs that lack the lanolin odor and weight.

Dyes in Mexican imitations are commercially produced and of a more consistently solid color, while those in authentic Navajo rugs may seem to streak. Study the grays. The Navajo combines black and white wool to create variations in color. Mexican grays are dull, light or dark, and uniform in color. Mexican produced reds are bright; the Ganado is a deep red.

Look closely at the weave. Mexican rugs are loosely woven compared to the tight weave of the Navajo. Often they have fringed ends that are rethreaded into the weave, making the fringe appear to be part of the original work. Navajo rugs, on the other hand, are woven to the ends. If a Navajo weaver produces fringe on the ends, it will be added onto the finished piece.

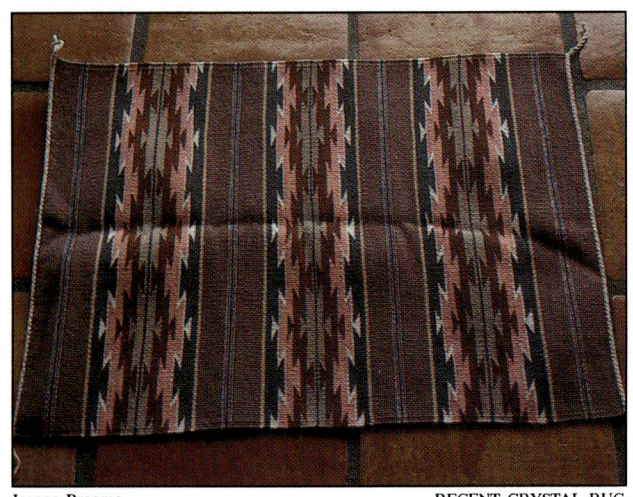

Jeanne Broome   RECENT CRYSTAL RUG

Basic Tips For Buying

1. Navajo rugs are handmade and therefore have small flaws. Perfection can be expected in machine made products.
2. The Navajo rug should be evenly woven and not curl when fully opened.
3. The Navajo weave should be tight with a uniform design from end to end. Corners should be tied off. Ends and borders should be straight with no warp threads showing.
4. Navajo rugs should be relatively smooth with no excessive lumping or thin areas.
5. Some color variances may be present in the Navajo rug but they should not be excessive.
6. Know the characteristics of Mexican imitations so you won't be fooled.
    * Dyes are commercially made and uniform in color.
    * Lighter in weight because of commercially produced yarns.
    * Reds are bright in Mexican rugs. Grays are dull, dark or light and uniform in color.
7. Always buy from reputable dealers. See p.47-8 for suggestions in locating a reliable dealer.

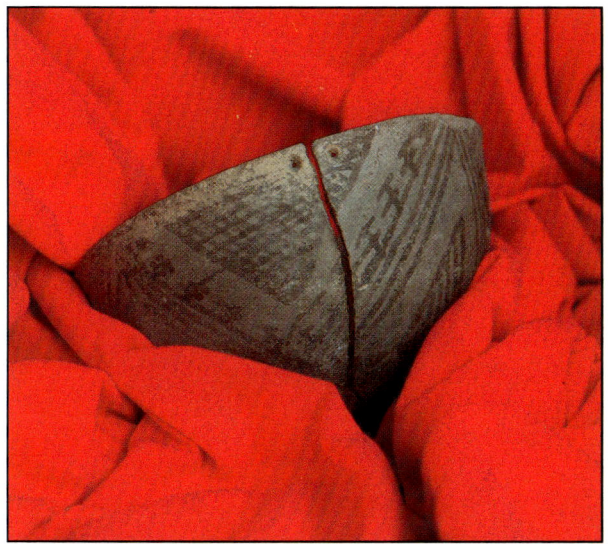

Jeanne Broome   HOHOKAM POT, FOUND BY DIFFERENT PEOPLE ON DIFFERENT DAYS

POTTERY, TODAY & YESTERDAY

"First Man and First Woman led the People into the new world. They came to a river and made some of the waters run on the land, planted the corn seeds they had brought with them and told their sons, the Changing Twins, to watch over the fields. One Twin saw some reeds growing near the river. He picked them and wove them into a water basket. The other Twin noticed some earth of a different color. He put some of the earth in the palm of his hand and it shaped into a bowl. Then, he formed a plate and a ladle."

A sense of mystery emerges when, walking along ancient Indian ground, you suddenly spot a potsherd. How old is it? Who made it? What is its color and design? Quickly you scour the area, hoping to find other pieces that might fit the pattern. Unfortunately, so many artifacts of the ancient potters have now been carried off to private collections or placed in museums that even potsherds are becoming scarce.

Ancient Indian Pottery

The Hohokam (HO-ho-kawm) people dwelled in what are now southern Arizona's desert valleys from about 300 B.C. to 1400 A.D. These ancestors of the Pima and Tohono O'odham cultivated farm crops and utilized the water from the Salt and Gila rivers for irrigation by engineering canal systems into their fields.

---

*From a Navajo myth

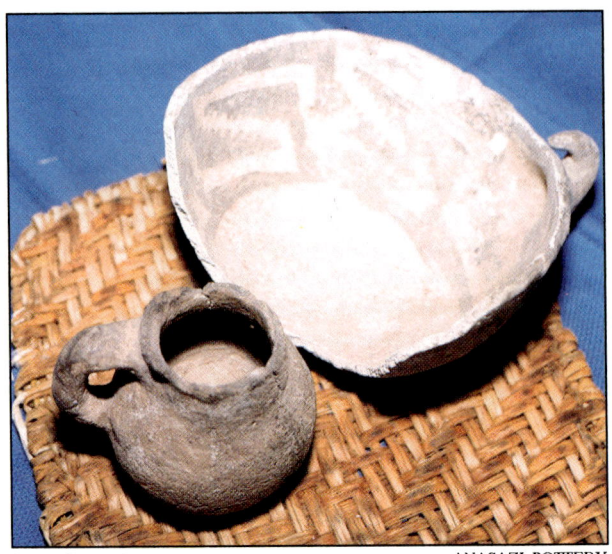

Jeanne Broome   ANASAZI POTTERY

Early southwest pottery dating from the third century B.C., has been found at these Hohokam sites. Showing skills of experienced potters, the pieces represent a craft probably learned from Mexican neighbors. Hohokam pottery is red-on-gray or red-on-buff, both with various geometric designs and life forms.

Living in the higher regions and valleys along the present Arizona/New Mexico border were the Mogollon (MUGGY-own). Mogollon pottery ranged from brown and red ware with geometric designs to red-on-white and black-on-white, with designs of fish, deer, birds, insects, and rabbits. The Mogollon eventually were assimilated into other groups. Their movement is traced north towards the White Mountains, where they encountered Anasazi, believed to be the ancestors of the Zuni, Hopi, and Rio Grande Pueblo people.

The earliest Anasazi were basket makers, but about the fifth century A.D. they began developing pottery. The often rough pieces indicate that these cliff dwellers developed their own methods of pottery making without the influence of the Hohokam or Mogollon. The Anasazi produced a variety of painted pottery including black-on-white, white ware and polychrome.

Unlike old world pottery of Asia, Europe and the Mediterranean, new world pottery was created without a potter's wheel, glazes, or kilns. Rich clay slips covered the surfaces rather than glazes. Vitreous glaze paints didn't appear in the Southwest until after 1000 A.D. With the exception of Mohave pottery, the term "style" refers to decorative style or the surface embellishment of an object, rather than shape or form.

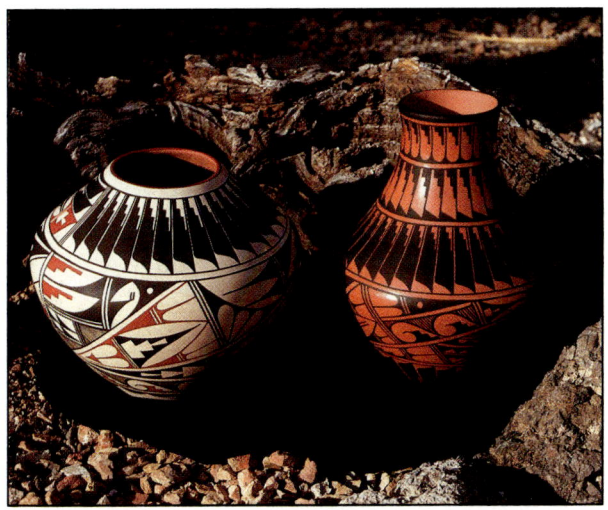

Jeanne Broome   JEMEZ POTTERY OF GERALDINE SANDIA

Modern Indian Pottery

Modern pottery, some fashioned closely after the ancient pieces of the Hohokam, Mogollon, and Anasazi, can be found in abundance in the Four Corners region. Today's pottery is a reflection of the ancestor mothers, aunts, and grandmothers who were the teachers. For example, some Jemez pottery is created using old Pecos Pueblo techniques. Mimbres pottery design is found in some Acoma creations.

The art of handmade pottery is generations old. What is contemporary today will be tradition tomorrow, as the rediscovery process goes on. In selecting the perfect piece of pottery, it's best to visit the pueblos and villages of the Southwest. While some pottery may be purchased for as little as $10, most Indian craftspeople are asking market value for their work. Pottery is important to the economic and social structure of many Indian communities.

Many steps in pottery making are done by hand. Clay is dug, placed in large buckets, and taken back to the pueblo for drying. Clay chunks are spread on sheets of tin and turned occasionally to permit even drying. On a hot day, drying takes a few hours.

After drying, the clay is soaked in a washtub for two to four days. Periodically the water is poured off and clean water added until it is clear. The potter then stirs the clay to form a soupy solution that is strained through a sieve made from a wooden frame and window screen. Clay rolls and particles that don't pass through the sieve are thrown away. None of the clay sludge is forced through the screen. The sifted clay is mixed with water to a milk shake consistency. Enough

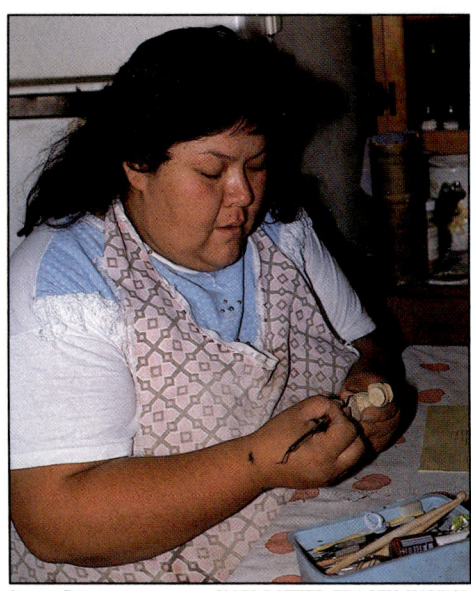

Jeanne Broome   HOPI POTTER TRACEY KOVINA
CARVING CORN MAIDEN

clay is prepared to last several days.

The tempering sand (called tuff) is also dug by hand. Potters sometimes travel 100 miles to find just the right kind. The tuff is worked through a sieve to break down the pieces into a fine powder. Clay and tuff are then mixed by hand (or foot!) on a piece of canvas until the desired putty-like texture is achieved. In preparation for the visitors' season, many potters will prepare enough clay for dozens of pieces at one time.

Pots are constructed on a lap board or table. The potter keeps water nearby to moisten both hands and tools, including modeling tools such as spoons, shaping and scraping tools, and a dish or basket to hold the base of the vessel. The spoons and shaping tools are usually handmade from natural items such as gourds or coconut shells. The latter remain hard and last longer than the gourd implements.

Ute Mountain Ute Pottery

In the extreme southwest corner of Colorado, Ute Mountain Utes create distinctive handmade pottery at the Ute Mountain Pottery Plant. Using commercially produced clay, the pottery is formed, cleaned and painted by Ute Mountain artists and artisans who work at the plant. Tribal members claim that the designs on each piece are one-of-a-kind, with each artist creating a distinctive style. Ute Mountain Pottery is sold wholesale directly from the plant or in retail shops.

POTTERY OF THE SOUTHWEST PUEBLOS

The Pueblo villages of the southwest cluster together in New Mexico from Taos in the north to Isleta, south of Albuquerque. To the west are Laguna, Acoma, and Zuni. The Hopis stand alone on their three mesas in northeastern Arizona. Pieces may be purchased directly from the individual potters at the various pueblos and in tribal cooperatives (see p.47-8), museum gift shops, and many Indian craft stores.

Taos and Picuris (TAH-ohs and Pee-CUR-is)

Located in northern New Mexico, the Taos and Picuris pueblos are famous for their shimmering, unpainted pottery. Formed from clay rich in mica, the pieces require no temper.

Taos pottery is simple, usually plain or with a single design, and gold in color. Picuris pots are often bronze or reddish orange. Shapes range from tall vases with round bottoms to bowls and bean pots with lids. Bean pots are used for cooking. To keep food from acquiring an earthy taste, potters waterproof the piece by sealing it with oil and heating in an oven. It's a good idea to place a copper or other metal heat absorber on the burner to protect the pot from direct heat.

Tewa Pueblos

Tewa speaking people occupy the region known as the Rio Grande Bad Lands between Espanola and Santa Fe, New Mexico. These pueblos include the San Juan, Santa Clara, San Ildefonso, Nambe, Pojoaque and Tesuque.

San Juan - The San Juan potters combine old and modern pottery styles. An incised middle band, copied from ancient pot sherds, is placed on a polished red rim and base of a micaceous slip made from thinned mica-impregnated clay. This produces a design that glitters. Other pottery will be unpolished in the middle between reds with polychrome designs. Shapes include pots, seed jars, plates, and cooking pots.

Santa Clara - One of many legends of the Santa Clara tells that during a drought, a bear led the people to water and the people now place its track on their work as a remembrance. In addition to the bear track, Santa Clara potters incorporate other symbols into their designs.

The water serpent represents liquid water such as

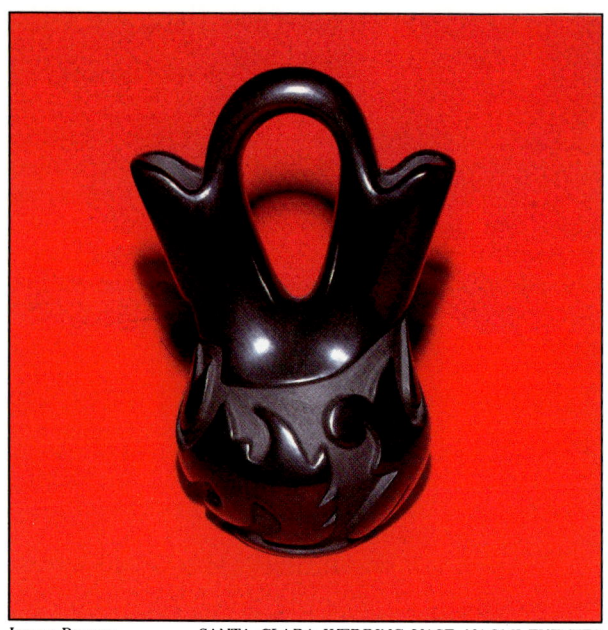
Jeanne Broome   SANTA CLARA WEDDING VASE, NAOMI FUENTES

rain, or streams and other bodies of water. Kiva steps representing the entrance into the ceremonial pit or kiva, add significant religious meaning to a piece. The feather design on pottery pieces shows respect for birds and is used in religious dances and ceremonies, for fanning smoke upon one being prayed over. The eagle represents nature's forces traveling the sky through wind and lightning. Rain and the rainbow symbolize the strong winds carrying storms.

Santa Clara potters use earth tones--yellow or buff, red, white, gray, and matte black on the polished blackware. Blackware, created by the Santa Clara and San Ildefonso potters has a 300-year history. The shiny pottery, often marked with the Santa Clara bear paw design, is fired in manure-smothered blazes, giving it the jet black finish. It was from this old method that Julian Martinez, husband to the famous Maria of San Ildefonso, created his matte blackware.

Shapes include the wedding vase, a double-spouted strap-handled wedding jar, plates, and blackware animals. Besides red and blackware, polychrome, sgraffito, miniatures and "clay people" are also created. Pottery is an important economic and social base of Santa Clara society.

San Ildefonso is home of the famous Maria Martinez and those craftspeople who trained under her watchful eye. San Ildefonso Pueblo Indians create pottery so unique that when she was younger Maria is said to have

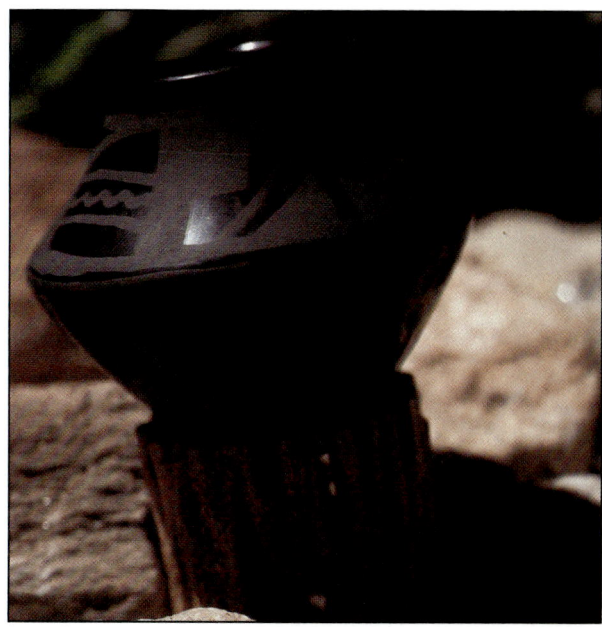

Jeanne Broome SAN ILDEFONSO POT, ALICE MARTINEZ

signed almost any well-made blackware. Matte black painted on the highly polished jet black finish remains Maria's legacy to the San Ildefonso people.

The water serpent, which also represents rain, thanksgiving and a prayer for water, is a San Ildefonso trademark. Sgraffito pots, two-toned red, polychrome, carved pottery, black matte, and red and blackware are all produced in San Ildefonso.

Nambe and Pojoaque - Very little pottery has been produced at Nambe Pueblo since the turn of the century. But in the early 1980s several potters moved from Nambe to Pojoaque and produced a variety of ceramic figures. Among them were storytellers-- charming figures surrounded by children--like those created in the Cochiti pueblo (pg.36), along with small jars and wedding vases.

Tesuque - Storytellers, black-on-white pottery, polychrome, nativity sets, and rain gods--figures produced expressly for the tourist trade--are made at Tesuque. Potters from this pueblo, among them Lorencita Pino, Manuel Vigil, Joseph B. Pino, and Anna Marie Lovato, are well-known for the Tesuque rain gods. In addition, they produce fine polychrome vessels. Storytellers are distinguished by their bright colors, children clinging to the adult figure, and rabbit-fur adornment.

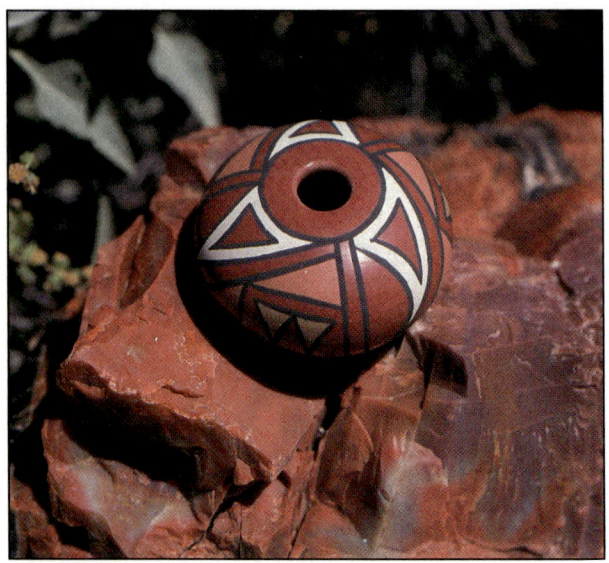

Jeanne Broome   POJOAQUE WEED POT, JOE & THELMA TALACHY

Middle Rio Grande Pueblos

Located west and southwest of Santa Fe and scattered on both sides of I-25 to a point south of Albuquerque are the Middle Rio Grande Pueblos. They include Cochiti, Santo Domingo, San Felipe, Sandia, Jemez, Zia and Santa Ana. A few potters produce work at San Felipe and Sandia pueblos.

Cochiti - A quarter of the more than 200 Pueblo potters who make figurative pottery are Cochiti. The famous "Storytellers" were first created by Helen Cordero in 1964. Helen remembered her grandfather who always had many grandchildren around him when he told stories, and she fashioned the figures in his memory. Her first storyteller had five children hanging from the seated grandfather whose eyes are closed in thought and whose mouth is open in song. Others of Helen's figures include a drummer, Navajo storytellers, a turtle taking children for a ride, and the "children's hour," showing older youth grouped around the storyteller.

Santo Domingo - Simple, bold geometrics as well as birds and flowers adorn the pottery from Santo Domingo. But Santo Domingo religious leaders forbid painting human figures and other sacred designs on pottery made for sale. Unlike the Zia birds (p. 37) which are jumping or flying, Santo Domingo birds are usually in still life. Pots are still used for cooking, dough preparation, and storage by the native people.

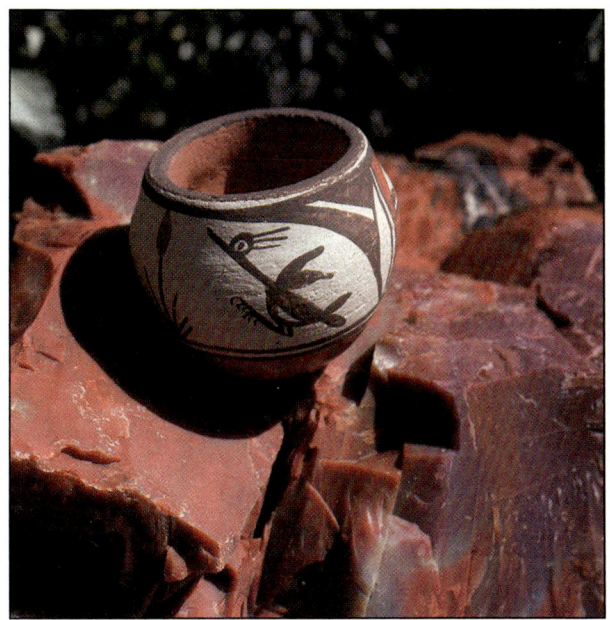

Jeanne Broome ZIA POT BY GLORIA G.

Zia - Zia potters are the only ones who temper their clay with basalt, a volcanic rock which creates a very hard pot. The pottery is stone polished and painted with black pigment. Common Zia designs include feathers, prayer sticks, (used in ceremonies for special prayers and bidding), spiderwebs, clouds, lightning and birds. The Zia bird, this peoples' hallmark, resembles a roadrunner, sacred for its speed and a bearer of prayers. The New Mexico state symbol, a stylized sun, came from an old Zia ceremonial pot.

Santa Ana - Old Santa Ana style potters create with a river sand temper using historic designs of clouds, circles called "turkey eyes," horses and human figures. The pueblo is no longer occupied but the Santa Ana live on nearby farms and a few continue to make pottery.

Jemez - Here the collector will find soft colors in pottery and figurines. The Pecos painted pottery of Jemez is indicative of the ancestrial Pecos pueblo. The Pecos people are said to have joined their linguistic relatives at Jemez in 1838 after abandoning their own pueblo.

The Pecos techniques studied by Evelyn Vigil, a Jemez potter, have become her trademark. Designs are painted on red clay pots with lead-based paint which

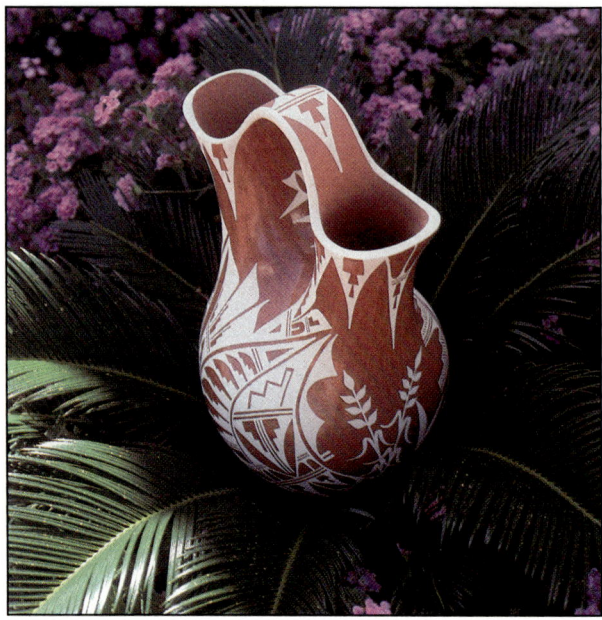

Jeanne Broome   JEMEZ WEDDING VASE, G. SANDIA

melts to a shining glaze after firing. Vigil is like all Jemez potters who invent as they create. The results range from intricately carved jars to painted bowls and pottery figures.

Acoma-Laguna-Isleta Region

Acoma - The Acoma Indian communities of Acomita, San Fidel, and McCartys are located near I-40 on the New Mexico Rio San Jose floodplain. Acoma clay is dark, nearly as dense as shale, and must be ground into a fine powder before it is mixed with temper. Famous for their thin, hard-fired walls, Acoma pots and jars are stone polished and painted with complex polychrome abstractions, red swirling bands, flowers, and parrots. Parrots, powerful symbols to the Acoma, may represent the south and sun, or ancestors. The potter may not think about meanings, rather will paint the parrot because it's the way of the people. The color red represents summer, sun and fertility.

Mimbres-style animals, named for people who settled in the Mimbres Valley in southwestern New Mexico (A.D. 950-1150), represent lizards, insects and animals intricately surrounded by tiny-lined stripes, feathers and other patterns. In recent years, These have become synonymous with Acoma pottery.

Laguna and Isleta - Prior to 1830, Laguna pottery was similar to that of the Acoma. Laguna variations of

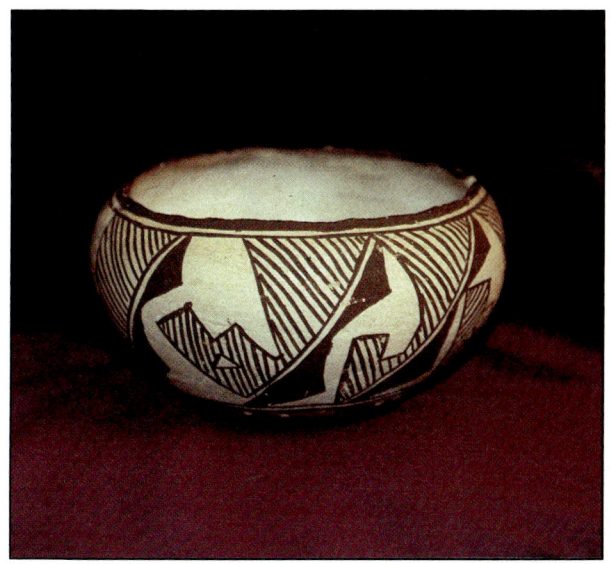

Charlotte Neyland — ACOMA BOWL

white-slipped polychrome decorated with boldly painted, simple designs were developed after that time.

Modern potter, Gladys Paquin, creates pottery by copying old Laguna methods of designing from personal inspiration. From her Christian training, she designs pottery with symbols representing her religious beliefs. The butterfly means new life; the worm, a change from her old to new self; and stair steps, the new dimension she found.

Stella Teller, another Isleta potter, also creates by inspiration. She paints with white slips over pastel tones. She also uses turquoise inlay (set into the clay) for contrast. Teller's figurines include the nativity scene and corn dolls--small figures shaped like ears of corn.

Zuni Fetishes

These carved stone or pottery pieces are crafted in the shape of living things, usually animals. All southwest tribes use them, but the Zunis are the greatest crafters of them.

Fetishes represent one phase of religious observances. They may belong to an individual, a secret society, a clan or an entire tribe. Thought to bring good luck, a fetish, if treated properly, is believed to help or give power to its possessor. Power is said to reside in the spirit dwelling within the fetish, not in the fetish itself. Figures of horses, cattle, and sheep, for example, are thought to protect these animals from disease and ensure propagation. Beware: Some fetish necklaces are imported in quantity from Italy and Mexico.

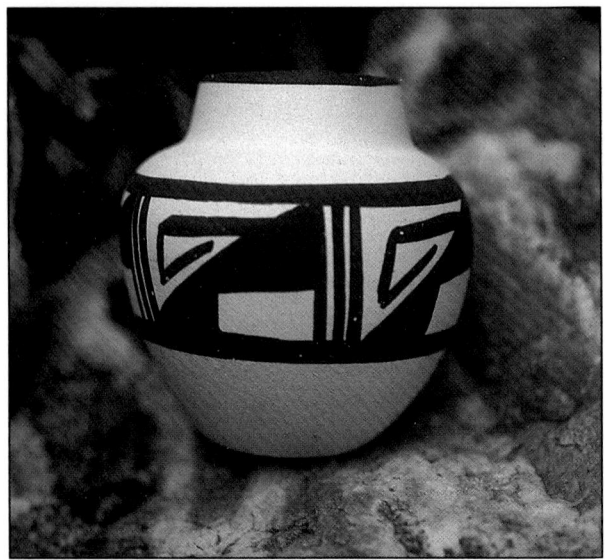

Jeanne Broome   COLORADO UTE BOWL

WHAT MAKES A PIECE OF POTTERY VALUABLE?

Valuable Indian pottery comes from the care, time, effort and personal relationship to the craft that a potter puts into creating a piece. While a few potters may simply paint on purchased greenware, most dig and prepare their clay and form the pieces with great concern for the finished product. Here are some guidelines for selecting quality creations:

* The interior and exterior should be symmetrical and smooth, free of pits or lumps.
* The surface should show no polishing stone grooves.
* Designs should be evenly spaced and outlines uniform. Painted strokes on the filled areas should cover the entire slip underneath.
* Carvings should be the same depth throughout the piece.
* No black smudges should appear on redware. No buff areas on blackware.
* Signed pieces can be an indication of high quality, but some of the greatest potters do not sign their work.

Prices may range from $10 for a miniature bowl to several hundred dollars for large pieces. Like buying any treasure, it's best to shop around before you make your final selection.

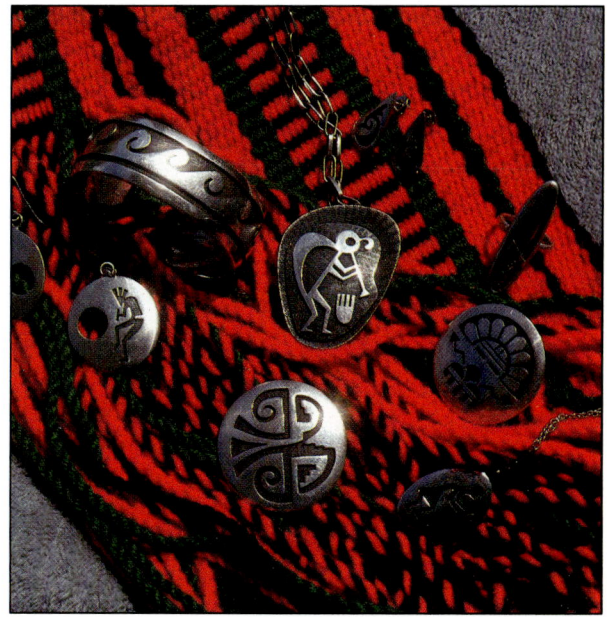

Jeanne Broome   HOPI SILVER OVERLAY ON HOPI BELT

JEWELRY

"The First People came up to the world after it was ready, and they moved around the edge of the world clockwise. There were birds and animals and trees, but no people. Each of these beings became a different tribe. As the world turned different ones of these animals or birds or trees stepped off. After several others had found places that they liked and had begun to make their homes, the alligator-barked Juniper said, 'I shall live here.' He was wearing turquoise beads, and they became his berries. Later another of the junipers found a home. He also had on turquoise beads, and he still wears them. Another of the juniper people stopped next. He selected his place and stands there still, wearing his turquoise beads."*

Indian jewelry appears today throughout the United States and in countries abroad. To some it is just jewelry, but to those who understand the artistry or have the privilege of watching an Indian silversmith at work, the pieces bear an extra special meaning.

In this day of mass producing and imitation, travelers to the Southwest may be fooled by jewelry said to be Indian made. Indians do not create by mass production. Each piece is unique. Only those pieces that come in pairs such as earrings, belt conchas or rows of beads will be alike. Production jewelry was

---

*A Lipan Apache myth

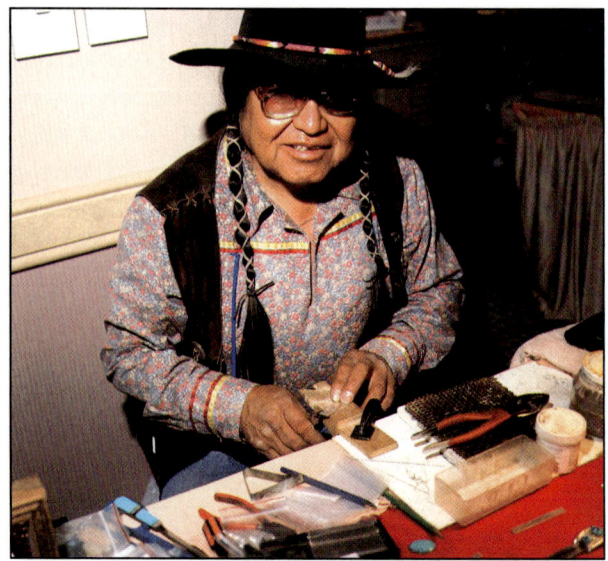

Jeanne Broome   NAVAJO SILVERSMITH JOE BEGAY

once assembled and soldered by Indians and called "Indian made," but the elements and parts were stamped out on machines by the thousands. But this practice was declared illegal in the 1930s.

The tools used by Indian silversmiths are similar in each tribe and essential for the creation of the unique pieces. The work table upon which the metal is heated is made of stone, metal or broken pottery, and cemented together with adobe. For soldering, the jeweler uses a blowtorch or an acetylene torch. An anvil and hand tools such as shears, snips, pliers, tweezers, hammers, mallets, a vise, dies, and punches complete the artist's equipment.

Although sterling silver is used today, Indians of the early 1900s preferred Mexican coin silver acquired through trading. The early pesos were a fine grade of silver, but after 1940 they were made of a lower grade. Today's sterling (an alloy) is acquired in sheet and wire form of 925 parts pure silver and 75 parts copper. Pure silver is too soft for ordinary jewelry work.

Navajo

Navajo metalsmiths first worked with iron making bridle bits. Atsidi Sani ("Old Smith"), a medicine man, learned metal work at Vallencitas, a Mexican settlement near Mount Taylor in what is now New Mexico. Said to be the first Navajo to work metal, he created knife blades, bits, and bridle parts. He passed his knowledge on to his four sons who sold bits around the country. More Navajos learned to work the black metal and

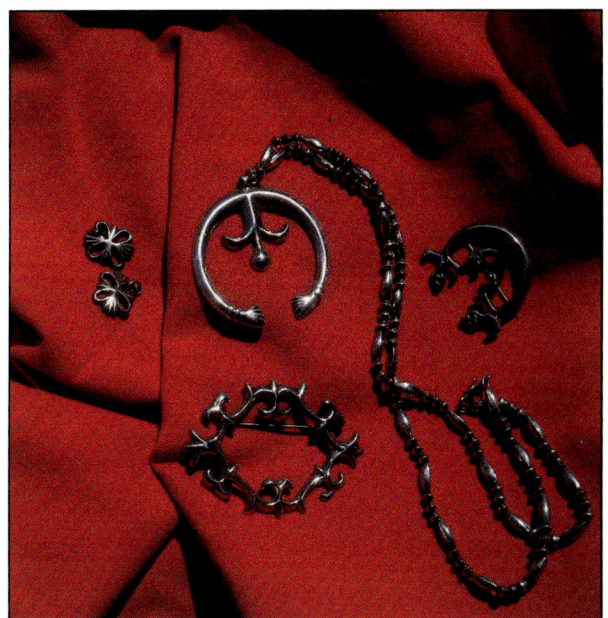

Jeanne Broome   NAVAJO CAST SILVER & BEADWORK

became known as professional blacksmiths.

The working of copper and then silver--called "metal of the moon"--followed. The natives also learned silver work from the Mexicans. Although these traveling artisans guarded their skills, the Navajos picked up the techniques. Early silver work adorned trousers, jackets, and moccasins in the form of buttons made from silver dollars. These were also applied to belts, gun scabbards, saddles, bridles, and bow guards. Casting was done by melting several coins and either hammering a cast ingot into a sheet of metal or pouring the molten silver into a carved mold.

Certain forms predominate in the styles of the Indian tribes. Old Navajo pieces, for example, are primarily silver, made with large, single stones such as turquoise, agate, petrified wood, and coral. With a few exceptions, Navajo smiths do not create inlay work, made by laying the stone or shell into silver.

Symmetrical in design, traditional Navajo jewelry is begun in the center of the piece and completed out toward the edges. Each piece is perfectly balanced horizontally and vertically, and there is little repetition in the pattern. Navajo designs do not translate symbolically or religiously. Some early bracelet designs represented animals, but those were rare.

Zuni

Like the Navajos, the Zunis began their metal

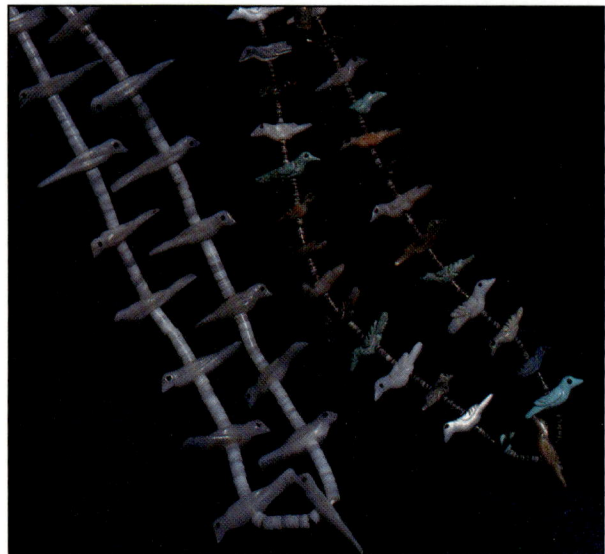

Jeanne Broome   ZUNI FETISH NECKLACES

working with iron. Copper and brass work came next, preceding their use of silver. Lanyade, a Zuni silversmith, learned from the Navajo medicine man, Atsidi Sani, who set up a workshop at his house to make silver ornaments, bridles and belts. Lanyade in turn, taught a smith named Balawade who passed the craft on to others. Gradually the craftsmen learned silver work and began incorporating turquoise, coral and other stones into the pieces.

The Zuni are now considered the most accomplished jewelers of all American Indian tribes. Zuni silver is usually constructed rather than cast. Because of the work they put into the design and stone cutting, the Zuni smiths are recognized as lapidaries. Zuni workmanship surpasses that of their Navajo neighbors, primarily because of their use of stones. A number of characteristic styles have been mastered by Zuni smiths. Among them are:

Clusters--small stones, often in rows, which form bracelets, belts, rings, earrings, and brooches.

Needlepoint--multiple, minute cabochons with sharply pointed ends are set in straight or curved lines. The stones are matched for color and shape.

Petit Point, a modified version of needlepoint, uses teardrop-shaped stones. Although some dealers refer to this as needlepoint, any piece containing this shape is petit point.

Mosaics of turquoise, shell, coral, and countless other stones--even nuts--are arranged to form multicolored, regular and irregular outlines. Many designs represent animals, birds, or insects. Some have religious associations such as the kachina, sun shield, or ritual dancers.

Channel work (the name given to a Navajo and Zuni art form) is inlaid stones in shared bezels. Each stone is cut and cemented, ground and polished to produce a smooth, shining surface on a continuous plane.

Hopi

The Hopi began working in silver prior to 1900, learning the craft from the Zuni smith Lanyade. He, like other smiths, is said to have traveled to Hopiland to make silver to sell. He guarded his trade, but at least one person--his host, Sikyatala *(SIKYA-tala)*--did observe. Sikyatala became sufficiently skilled and sold his wares to trader Tom Keam and to other Hopis on First Mesa.

The success of Hopi silversmiths today is due largely to Doctor Harold S. Colton and his wife, Mary Russell-Ferrell Colton, founders of the Museum of Northern Arizona at Flagstaff. They encouraged the natives to produce Hopi jewelry, not imitations of Navajo, and to develop their own designs. In 1947, silversmithing classes were started where craftsmen perfected their designs and the art of silver overlay. The matte black background became a basic part of Hopi design at New Oraibi, midway through the 20th century.

Hopi silver jewelry designs depend strictly upon the artist's skill and inspiration. They can be realistic, as in a depiction of a kachina, or they can be a very simple stylized design. Rain, clouds, corn plants, and feathers are a few of the elements represented in Hopi silver.

The best way to learn about the piece you select is to ask the silversmith. A number of Hopi smiths have their own shops where you can observe their work and select from their finished pieces.

Hallmarks are used by many Hopi smiths to identify their work. They may be the smith's initials or a symbol indicative of the person's clan. Michael Sockyma on Second Mesa stamps his initials within the mound upon which a stalk of corn, representing the Young Corn Clan, is placed. Other smiths use no hallmark, some use only their initials or clan symbol, and still others make a mark that does not represent the clan. A good source for determining Hopi hallmarks is Margaret Wright's book *Hopi Silver*.

OTHER NATIVE CRAFTS

Navajo Sandpaintings

Navajo sandpainting is an intricate and sacred part of the spirituality of the people. Having no word for religion in their language, the Navajo believe that all thinking, health, harmony, beauty, and spirituality are related. All life is seen as sacred. Religion is not a separate part of the belief system. Illness is thought to occur when a person is in disharmony with one or more aspects of life.

Sandpaintings, created by a healer specially trained in this art, are said to serve as pathways. They exchange an illness for the healing power of the Holy People, spiritual beings of the Navajo sacred beliefs. The sandpainting is created near the afflicted person and prayers are offered by the healer and other participants on his or her behalf. Through the power of the prayers the Holy People depicted in the sandpainting are believed to bring wellness in exchange for illness in the patient. Once the sandpainting is created and has served its purpose, it is destroyed as part of the final act of the healing ritual.

Commercialized sandpaintings may not be true representations of the real ones used for healing. Some are simply representations or pictures of actual Holy figures and plants used in healing rituals. Some of the true depictions are displayed at the Wheelwright Museum of the American Indian in Santa Fe, New Mexico. Sandpaintings may be purchased in many curio shops, trading posts, and galleries.

Kachina Dolls

Although the Hopi people are most noted for Kachina doll carvings, the Zuni also create and sell some which represent their ritual dancers. Kachinas are believed to be masked spirits of the invisible forces of life. Dressed in elaborate costumes and masks, men dance in annual ceremonial rituals representing the various spirits. The belief is that the spirit of a particular Kachina enters the dancer and for a time is present among the people.

Kachina dolls are made both for ceremonial use and public sale. Museums such as the Heard in Phoenix and the Arizona State Museum in Tucson have outstanding collections of Kachina dolls, some of which date from the late 19th century. Kachinas can be purchased in many trading posts, Indian art galleries, and curio shops.

Beadwork

One of the most colorful art forms of Southwest Indians is beadwork. While all tribes make beaded items for sale, some of the most notable are created by the Zuni and Ute. Zuni beadwork was at one time limited to beaded dolls. Today both men and women create ceremonial dance figures, animals, and storyteller figures from carved cottonwood, intricately covered with beads.

Modern Ute Indians live today on reservations in Colorado and Utah. The Ute Mountain and Southern Ute tribes are located in southwestern Colorado, while the Northern Ute inhabit the Uintah and Ouray reservation of eastern Utah. The Ute have done beadwork for many decades and continue to design leather clothing, moccasins, belts, bags, purses and pouches, each decorated with exquisite beadwork.

INDIAN ARTS & CRAFTS ASSOC.

The Indian Arts and Crafts Association (IACA) is a New Mexico based organization comprised of dealers throughout the country. Its purpose is to "enhance and maintain the image and marketing of handmade American Indian Arts and Crafts." Their code of ethics, which each participating dealer is required to display and follow, requires that the work be: "An honest representation of the nature and origin of American Indian arts and crafts; abiding by all Federal, state, local and tribal laws which pertain to the works, artifacts, and natural resources..."

IACA members are not obligated to sell only handmade Indian jewelry, but they are required to inform buyers of whether or not a piece is authentic and if the turquoise has been treated or stabilized and is not a pure art stone. IACA dealers must refund a buyer's money or apply the purchase price to another article if any item is found to have been misrepresented.

To learn more about the association's criteria for authenticity, write to the Ethics Committee and request a copy of the rules.

Indian Arts and Crafts Association
122 La Veta NE, Suite B
Albuquerque, NM 87301
(505) 265-9149

A complete list of general members can be obtained by writing for the Directory of Members and Buyers Guide. A few are listed on the following page.

TRIBAL ENTERPRISES, CO-OPS

Hopi Arts & Crafts Coop. Guild
P.O. Box 37
Second Mesa, AZ 86043-0037
(520)734-2463 (IACA Member)
Products: Art (two-dimensional including prints, posters), baskets, children's items, dolls, drums, pipes, jewelry, kachina dolls, miniatures, pottery, storytellers, nativity sets, weavings, wall hangings, repair, and restoration.

Navajo Arts & Crafts Enterprise
PO Box 160
Window Rock, AZ 86515
(520)871-4095,4090,2060
(IACA Member)
Products: Baskets, beadwork, dolls, dye charts (examples of vegetal dyes), fetishes, jewelry, navajo carvings of kachinas, pottery, storytellers, nativity sets, rugs, weavings, wall hangings, sandpaintings, sculpture, carvings, supplies, findings, stones, shells, repair, and restoration.

Pueblo of Zuni Arts and Crafts
P.O. Box 425
Zuni, NM 87327
(505)782-5531 (IACA Member)
Products: Art (two-dimensional including prints, posters), beadwork, children's items, Christmas ornaments, jewelry, fetishes, dolls, miniatures, pottery, storytellers, rugs, nativity sets, weavings, wall hangings, sculpture, carvings.

Gu-Achi District Enterprises
(Tohono O'Odham Indians
of Southern Arizona)
P.O. Box 398
Sells, AZ 85635
(520)361-2339
Products: Paintings, pottery, woodcrafts, Jewelry, baskets (wire, reed, horsehair, miniatures), and beadwork.

Sky Ute Indian Gallery
PO Box 737
Ignacio, CO 81137
(303)563-4649
Products: Art (two dimensional including prints, posters), beadwork, jewelry, pottery, storytellers, nativity sets, sandpaintings, sculpture, carvings, repair, restoration.

Indian Pueblo Cultural Center
2401 12th NW
Albuquerque, NM 87104
(505)843-7270
Products: Pottery, kachina dolls, sculptures, jewelry, rugs, sandpainting, drums, curio items, baskets, beadwork, art (two dimensional including prints.)

Cultural Rights Protection Office and Museum of the Northern Ute Tribe
PO Box 190
Hwy. 40, Bottle Hollow Complex
Fort Duchesne, UT 84026
(801)722-4992
Products: Art (two dimensional, beadwork including clothing, belts, purses, moccasins, pouches, jewelry and dolls.

Ute Mountain Pottery Plant
Highway 666
Towaoc, CO 81334
(303)565-8548
Products: Pottery

Navajo Tourism Department
PO Box 663
Window Rock, AZ 86515
(520)871-6436,7371

SELECTED MUSEUMS

Heard Museum of Anthropology & Primitive Art
22 E Monte Vista Road
Phoenix, AZ 85004

Arizona State Museum
University of Arizona campus
Tucson, AZ 85721

Utah Museum of Natural History
University of Utah
10th E Street
Salt Lake City, UT 84112

Museum of Northern Arizona
Route 4, Box 720
Flagstaff, AZ 86001

Wheelwright Museum of the American Indian
Old Santa Fe Trail
at Camino Lejo
Santa Fe, NM 87501

Indian Pueblo Cultural Center
2401 12th Street, NW
Albuquerque, NM 87102

Denver Museum of Natural History
2001 Colorado Boulevard
Denver, CO 80205